SHOP DESIGN SERIES

THE WORLD AIRPORTS

Yoichi Arai

International Airports & Their Commercial Facilities

Photos by Nacása & Partners

ヒューマン・エアポートの創造に向けて
新井洋一

空港は未来にいちばん近い都市

いま，われわれは，多くの分野で人類の歴史の新たな段階に入りつつあるという，大きな変化を体験しつつある。この新たな段階は，多くの人々から新たな時代の到来としてとらえられ，これまでの数百年の長い歴史をもつ「近代」と対比されようとしている。新たな時代を支えている変化の要素を，私は次の三つのキーワードとしてとらえてみたい。

「ヒューマナイズド」…近代の開発した合理性や効率性を引き継ぎつつ，人を主役とした，さらに豊かな人間性の回復の進展。

「エコロジカル」…自然や生態系との共生，協調の進展。

「トランス・ナショナル」…国家の概念を超えた，より広範で大量の個別的な結びつきと交流の進展。

このような変化は，近年の空港をめぐる大きな変化と重なっており，空港は，新たな時代を拓き支える，最も先導的な施設としてとらえられよう。

空路による人々の移動が始まって，まだ歴史は浅い。しかし，いまや年間，定期便で移動した国際線の乗客だけで，3億2000万人（IATA，1993年）を数え，さらにその数は，年々5％以上の率で伸びていくと推計されている。

空路による人々の移動が，グローバルな広がりでの新たな時代を支えているのである。

また空港それ自体も，単に乗客が乗り降りする通過空間ではなく，地域の都市構造の一部として，貿易や産業，研究や文化の中枢機能を強めつつある。

空港は，航空輸送システムの面では，グローバルな広がりであると同時に，地域の都市システムの一部として，ローカルな存在でもある。また，周辺との協調をめざしたエコロジカルな存在も追求されている。

さらに，空港内部に関しては，最先端の情報システムや輸送システムをもった，硬い巨大な精密機械であると同時に，人が主役の，ヒューマナイズドな，柔らかな有機的システムも，あわせもち始めている。

空港は，新たな時代の変化を最も敏感に受け止める，まさに先端都市そのもの，未来にいちばん近い都市空間としてとらえられよう。

私は，このような新たな特性をもつ空港を，「ヒューマン・エアポート」と呼び，概念づけたいと思う。

ヒューマン・エアポートの胎動

新たな空港時代の到来を予感させる，新しいコンセプトと空間をもった空港，「ヒューマン・エアポート」が，いま陸続と世界に誕生している。

日本では一昨年，国内初の24時間空港，海上空港として，関西国際空港がオープンした。

沖合に人工島をつくり，世界的にも画期的な，騒音問題のない空港を実現した。また，周辺の自然環境への負荷を極力抑えた開発と運営の手法は，「エコロジカル」な空港のモデルとして高く評価されている。

空港経営の点で常に先鞭をつけてきたフランクフルト空港は，先頃第2ターミナルをオープンさせ，よりいっそう高度な都市機能を取り込んだ「空港都市」の実現をめざしている。空港施設を始め，ホテルや会議センターなどすべてを一つ屋根の下に集約。商業施設は日用品から高級品まで，圧倒的な集積を誇る。また，空港鉄道駅からフランクフルト中央駅までは10数分でアクセスが可能だ。今世紀中にさらにもう一つ駅を新設し，高速新幹線を運行する。

旅客を"パッセンジャー"ではなく"ゲスト"と呼んだ最初の空港，コペンハーゲン空港は，まさに「人を主役」に据えた，施設の整備と空港運営を展開している。ゲストに最善の施設とサービスを提供することにより，コペンハーゲン空港は大きく発展しつつある。

これらはほんの一例であるが，いま，世界の先

TOWARD THE CREATION OF HUMAN AIRPORTS
Yoich Arai

THE AIRPORT COMPLEX IS CLOSEST TO THE CITY OF THE FUTURE.

We are now experiencing significant changes in various disciplines as we move into a new stage of human history. Many view this new stage as the coming of a new era comparable to our modern age, which has lasted several hundred years. The fundamental elements of change may be summarized into three concepts.

"Humanized" —While maintaining the rationality and efficiency of the modern age, human beings will play the leading role in recovering humanity. "Ecological" —Enhancement of harmony with nature and the ecosystem. "Transnational" —More and varied exchanges and links among peoples and groups in the world beyond national boundaries.

The characteristics of the new era are evident in the modern airport complex, and it may be regarded as part of the vanguard of this era. While the history of aviation is brief, a recent survey shows that the number of passengers travelling on scheduled international flights alone has grown to more than 320 million per year(IATA,1993). It is estimated that this number will increase by more than 5% every year.

Increased air travel is making the new era a truly global phenomenon. The airport is no longer simply a transit space for landing and boarding. It is also being required to play a central role in trade, industry, research and culture, thus forming an integral part of a region's urban structure.

The airport is not only a node in international air transportation system, but it is also an important element of any local urban system. And it must perform its diverse functions while maintaining an ecological awareness of its natural surroundings.

The airport complex, itself, is a huge, fixed precision mechanism with state-of-the-art systems for information, baggage handling, and passenger transport; but at the same time, it has also begun to develop aspects of a flexible, humanized organism.

The airport complexes which reflect these changes most sensitively may be considered representative of what we can expect of future trends in airport design. And these are the airports we will refer to as "human airports."

HUMAN AIRPORTS COMING TO LIFE

Human airports with a new type of concept and space are being built at a rapid pace in anticipation of this new era.

In Japan, Kansai International Airport, a sea airport, was opened in 1994 as Japan's first airport to operate around the clock. Situated on a man-made island four kilometers offshore, it is an epoch-making airport without noise problems. Through its sound development and management policies, Kansai International has minimized any adverse impact on its natural surroundings. It has won high praise as the model of an ecologically sensitive airport.

Frankfurt Airport, a pioneer in airport management, recently opened its second terminal. It aims to create an "airport city" with sophisticated urban functions.The airport facilities, a hotel and convention centers are all housed under one roof.The retail shops boast a remarkable abundance of merchandise, with everything from everyday necessities to the finest of luxury items. Railway access is also excellent, with the airport being only a 12-minute ride from Frankfurt's central station. A second airport train station will be opened before the 21st century, and it will be served by Germany's superexpress network.
At Copenhagen Airport, passengers are called

進空港はいずれも「ヒューマン・エアポート」の創造をめざし、その実現のために努力を続けている。

空港の歴史的発展と新世代の空港

振り返ってみると、空港はおおよそ3期の発展段階を経て現在に至っている。

「第1期」は、空港の揺籃期で、1920〜40年代中期にあたる。1919年のパリ条約によって国際航空輸送の歴史が始まり、30年代以降、航空会社が相次いで設立された。この時代の国際空港は空港というよりは、軍事・物資輸送基地としての色合いが濃く、滑走路など離着陸の施設のみが備えられた、「飛行場」の名にふさわしいものであった。ここでの主役は「飛行機」もしくは「パイロット」である。

「第2期」は、国際空港の拡大発展期で、年代は1940〜1980年。第二次大戦後、国際航空路線の発達と航空輸送の増大化と、航空機の大型化により、旅客・貨物の輸送が急増。これに対応して空港も単なる飛行機の発着点という存在から、多くの人や物が集散する場所「空港」へと変貌していった。ことに1950年代に始まった本格的ジェット機時代は「空の大衆化」を促し、空港は増大する旅客のニーズに応えるため、レストランや売店など各種施設を設置するようになった。ここでの主役は「エアライン」である。

「第3期」は、いま胎動しつつある新世代の空港、「ヒューマン・エアポート」の時代であり、1990年代から21世紀へ向けて、空港がめざすべき姿である。「ヒューマン・エアポート」の特性とは何か。

第一に、「主役は人」である。空港計画や運営は人間を中心に据えて行われるだろう。

第二に、「地域との協調」である。空港はローカル・アイデンティティの体現者として、その地域や国の文化・歴史・産業等を広く内外にアピールするとともに、地域発展の牽引車として、また新たな空港都市として、より大きな経済的・社会的効果を地域にもたらしていくだろう。

第三に、「エコロジカル」な空港である。いま人類にとって最大の問題であるエコロジーへの対応は、空港にとっても必須の課題である。

「ヒューマン・エアポート」は、この三つを命題として、未来に一番近い都市の概念を重ねつつ、計画論においても経営理念においても、追求されていかなければならない。

世界の先進空港の経営コンセプト

「ヒューマン・エアポート」の実現に意欲的で、経営的にも成功をおさめている世界の先進空港の

うち、今回、本書のために解説を寄せていただいた空港の中から、いくつか興味深い経営の理念あるいは運営の目標を、担当者の言葉を借りて紹介したいと思う。

常に世界の"ベスト・エアポート"と高い評価を受けているシンガポール・チャンギ空港は、「私たちはちょうど、多くの楽器を抱えたオーケストラで一つのハーモニーをつくり出す指揮者のような存在です」と、空港経営の練達として、いわば奥義を述べている。

世界最大の旅客数を誇り"世界一多忙な空港"といわれるシカゴ・オヘア空港は、「次の事柄を心に刻み公共に奉仕することを約束します——安全と保護、顧客サービスと利用者の親しみ、環境的責任、清潔、運営と費用の効率——私たちの任務は、地域で、国内で、世界で選ばれた空港として前進することであり、また地域への経済的効果を拡張させていくことにあります」と、前述したヒューマン・エアポートの三つの命題をすべていい含んでいる。

空港の"人間化"にいち早く取り組んだコペンハーゲン空港は、「基本的理念は、この空港に1500万人の旅客ではなく、1500万人のゲストが訪れるということです。私たちは次の三つのサービスの理念を掲げています。"空港らしくない空港""あなたが満足するように""何のトラブルも起きない"——哲学的アプローチを思わせるこれらの理念は、空港の建物のデザインから小さな事柄の隅々に至るまで、あらゆるところで観察されます」と述べている。ちなみに、"空港らしくない空港"とは、あたかも巨大な機械のような空港を、快適でリラックスできる人間的な空港へとするために環境整備を図っていることをいう。"あなたが満足するように"とは、旅客それぞれのニーズに細やかに的確に対応していること、"何のトラブルも起きない"とは、「旅客一人の問題はわれわれ全員の問題」というモットーで、旅客の安心・安全の維持に努めていることをいっている。

満足・収入・協調の極大化

各空港の経営理念、運営目標を通観すると、「ヒューマン・エアポート」をめざす空港は、「満足・収入・協調」の三つの要素のハーモニーが必要だと結論づけられるのではないだろうか。

「利用客の満足の極大化」「空港の収入の極大化」「地域との協調の極大化」、これらが地域の別や空港の大小にかかわらず、全ての空港に課せられる最終の目標となろう。

guests. " People always come first" in the management and facilities improvement of Copenhagen Airport. By providing the best facilities and services to its guests, Copenhagen Airport is making remarkable progress.

These are a few examples. Every international airport in the world is striving to become a "human airport."

HISTORICAL DEVELOPMENT OF THE AIRPORT AND THE NEW-GENERATION AIRPORT—HUMAN AIRPORT

The airport has developed in three stages.The first stage spans a period from 1920 to mid '40s, when the airport was in its infancy. In 1919, the history of international transportation commenced with the Pact of Paris. After 1930, airlines were set up one after another. During this period, the airport was not much more than a base for air transport of military and civilian goods, with facilities only for taking off and landing. It was a "air field" in the true sense. Airplanes and pilots played a central role at this stage.

The second stage, from the 1940s to '80s, was the age of expansion and development of international airports. After the Second World War, international air routes increased and the air transportation grew. Large-scale aircraft were introduced and the passenger and cargo volume spiraled. From simply being a site for take-offs and landings, the airport was transformed into a facility where people gathered and vast quantities of cargo were collected and distributed. With the advent of the jet age in 1950s, air travel became even more popular, and airports began to offer passenger services such as restaurants and retail shops. During this period of airport development, the airlines played a major role.

The third stage, the age of the new-generation airport, the human airport, began in the 1990s and will continue into the 21st century.

What are the characteristics of the human airport? First,"people are its primary concern."Airport planning and management are developed according to this principle.Second, it strives to achieve "harmony with the region"and is regarded as a landmark,representing the local culture, history and industries. It will bring about large-scale economic expansion and social development. Finally, it is "ecologically conscious." One of the most serious problems ever faced by humanity—coping with ecological issues—is a critical issue for the human airport.

The human airport, being closest to the city of the future, must achieve these three goals in its policy-planning and management.

MANAGEMENT CONCEPT OF THE WORLD'S LEADING AIRPORTS

The world's leading airports introduced in this publication are both enthusiastic and successful in creating and managing human airports.Following are comments, from the management staff of some of these airports,regarding their operating principles and goals.

Singapore Changi Airport is constantly winning high praise as the world's best airport. Their staff say they are "like a conductor orchestrating many instruments into one harmonious whole." The message expresses the spirit of human airport management.

Management at Chicago O'Hare International, which boasts the world's biggest passenger volume, says, "we are commited to serving the public by making Chicago's airport system the world's best in safety and security, customer service and user friendliness, environmental responsibility, cleanliness, and efficiency of operations and cost. Our mission is to promote O'Hare as the airport of choice in the region, the United States and worldwide, and to expand our employment and our economic importance in the community." This comment touches on all three characteristics described above.

Copenhagen Airport is one of the leaders in the human airport movement. Its management says, "Our basic operating principle is: we don't have 15 million passengers every year, we are visited by 15 million guests every year. We have three concepts in service—*the non-airport airport, do as you please* and *no problem*". These concepts are apparent in the small details of the airport's operation and even in the airport's design.

Note, that, on this principle of *the non-airport airport,* Copenhagen Airport has been transformed from a huge machine-like complex into a comfortable and relaxed human space. *Do as you please* represents the management's desire to meet the individual needs of guests. *No problem* represents the motto of the airport's security

●利用客の満足の極大化

空港は基本的にはサービス産業とみなすことができ，商業空間としてのハード，ソフトを充足させていくことが肝要である。そうした視点でみると，今後は，旅客支援のための機能，旅行演出のための機能，空港内ビジネス開発のための機能，国際交流のための機能など，様々な都市的機能をさらに積極的，意欲的に開発，集積していくことが必要だろう。

もちろん，空港の基本的な機能である，旅客のスムーズで快適な移動についても，利用者の特性に対応して，よりいっそうの追求がなされるべきである。

●空港の収入の極大化

空港は複合的なサービス産業であり，経営の視点，競争力の維持は不可欠である。端的にいえば「儲かる空港」にしなければならない。

空港収入は，着陸料などの「航空収入」と，それ以外の「非航空収入」の二つの部門に分けられるが，このうち非航空収入の比重を上げることが，世界の空港の趨勢となっている。非航空収入と航空収入の割合は，例えばチャンギ空港では，68：32（1992年度），スキポール空港では，56：44（1992年）となっている。日本では，新東京国際空港が32：68（1993年度），関西国際空港が59：41（1994年度）である。

世界の空港は，安い着陸料でエアラインの乗り入れを促し，それにより空港利用者を増加させ，ひいては非航空収入を増加させようという戦略なのだ。

近年，顧客ニーズの多様化や空港機能の高度化が著しく，空港が再投資を迫られる機会が多くなっている。そのため空港収入を上げて，次の投資に備えることが必要だ。それを怠れば，新たな開発計画も実行できず，空港自体が陳腐化してしまうだろう。

●地域との協調の極大化

空港はよき隣人であるべきだ。母都市，周辺都市との連携・協調が必要である。

まずエコロジカルな観点では，騒音問題の解決や生態系との共生，景観・風景との調和が大きな要素となっていこう。

次に交通体系の観点では，母都市との多重で多様なアクセス手段の確保が必要である。

さらに都市機能の観点では，空港と地域の経済・社会・文化等との結びつきがより強まってこよう。空港を支援する産業や施設，あるいは立地のインパクトを地域発展に結びつけていく様々な施策，地域整備などが進められよう。

空港を単なる交通の結節点として考えるのではなく，新たな空港都市として，また地域発展の核として位置づけ，さらに，空港が地域の「誇り」や「アイデンティティ」の核となることが何より望まれよう。

アーティスティックなビジネス

「世界の空港で，成功している空港は一つもない」とはよくいわれることだ。これはある意味で当たっている。

私は，以前，高名な陶芸家がテレビでのインタビューにこたえて，自分の人生で未だ満足できる作品は一つも出来あがっていない，といっていたのを思い出す。

空港も，一つとして同じ空港はない，空港は一つ一つその表情を異にする，また，空港に要求される機能も時間とともに変化する。

空港づくりは，その大小にかかわらず，一つ一つが他に類例のないものの創造作業であり，空港の運営は，その毎日が同じく創造作業である。その意味で，空港の開発も運営も，きわめてアーティスティックな営為なのである。

一つの空港での試みが成功したからといって，その試みが他の空港で成功するとはかぎらない。このため，空港担当者に要求される資質としては，空港で起こることに対する，豊かな想像力をもつこと，さらには，それを集約して具体化していく強い実行力をもつこと，が挙げられよう。

このためには，どんな手立てがあるのだろうか。私は，その"カギ"はやはり，空港自体にあると考える。多くの空港の事例を研究すること，自分の空港をよく観察すること，また，多くの試みを実行すること，ではないだろうか。

哲学者・ヴィトゲンシュタインの言葉をかりれば"Nothing is hidden"，空港のことなら空港を，つまり，自分の足元を見つめることから始まり，すべてはここに尽きる，ということだ。

本書は，世界の空港の，主として「ヒューマナイズド」に視点をおいた，とりまとめとなっている。その作業に当たっては，世界の空港で，多くの試みを実行し，これを成功させているエキスパートの協力を得ている。これらの方々に感謝を述べるとともに，本書が，それぞれの空港のイメージを大きく広げ，新たな時代を拓いていくきっかけになることを願っている。

operation:"A guest's problem is every staff person's problem."

MAXIMIZATION OF SATISFACTION, REVENUE AND HARMONY

Management principles and goals of these airports demonstrate that the human airport is required to have three major elements- "maximum passenger satisfaction," "maximum revenue" and "maximum harmony with the region." These will be the ultimate goals of every human airport regardless of region or size.

MAXIMUM PASSENGER SATISFACTION

Since the airport business is essentially one of the service industries, it is important to have the qualities of a prosperous commercial space. In this regard, in additon to basic passenger support, airports are required to develop and upgrade urban functions aggressively, facilitating pleasant travels, providing facilities for business operations,and contributing to international communication.

It goes without saying that improvements in smooth and comfortable passenger movement, the basic function of the airport, must be made continually.

MAXIMUM AIRPORT REVENUE

As a complex service organization, the airport must have a clear management vision and a sense of competitiveness.The airport's revenues are divided into aviation revenues such as landing fees, and non-aviation revenues. The recent trend among world airports is to focus on increasing non-aviation revenues. Non-aviation revenues have increased to 68% of the total revenue at Changi Airport(1992), 56% at Schiphol(1992), 32% at New Tokyo International(1993) and 59% at Kansai International (1994). The major strategy is to attract more flights by offering lower landing fees, and thereby bring in more passengers and visitors.

As customer needs diversify and airport services become more sophisticated, reinvestment becomes not only increasingly important but also expensive. Unless the airports generate enough revenue to allow strategic reinvestment, they will become outdated and uncompetitive.

MAXIMUM HARMONY WITH THE REGION

An airport must be a good neighbor to its mother and surrounding cities. Ecologically,it is important to solve noise pollusion problems, coexist with the local ecosystem, and harmonize with the local landscape. As far as ground transport is concerned, the airport should have multiple and diverse access routes. With regard to urban functions, the linkage between the airport and its region's economy, community activities and culture will become stronger. Policies and local infrastructure must be improved to support the contribution of airport-related industries and facilities to the region. The airport is no longer a mere nodal point in transportation network. Instead, it should be evaluated as an airport city, or a nucleus of regional development. It is also hoped that the people in the region will take pride in it as a symbol of local identity.

ARTISTIC BUSINESS

It is often said that no airport in the world is successful. In a sense this is true. It is like a true artist being never satisfied with his/her work.

Every airport is different from other airports. The functions an airport is expected to fulfill also change with time. Regardless of size, building and improving an airport is a creative work, and no two airports are the same. Airport operation is also creative work, and changes from day to day. Both development and management are artistic processes.

The success of a particular idea or project at one airport does not guarantee success at another airport. The airport's management staff must be flexible and imaginative enough to cope with changing conditions, and dedicated enough to implement programs that are necessitated by new demands.

What can be done to obtain these qualities? The key is in the airport itself. Visit many airports and study each case closely, take a careful look at your own airport and put ideas and plans into practice.

Wittgenstein, an Austrian philosopher, says: "Nothing is hidden." That is, you look at yourself to find out about yourself. Similarly, everything that needs to be known about the airport must be apparent in the airport.

This book introduces leading "humanized" airports of the world, with the cooperation and assistance of their management staffs. The author is deeply grateful to these pioneers of the human airport. It is hoped that this publication will help broaden their perspective and make further innovations into the future.

目次　CONTENTS

THE WORLD
INTERNATIONAL
AIRPORTS

ハイレベルのサービスと十分なキャパシティを目指す

アムステルダム・スキポール空港

オランダ，アムステルダム

AMSTERDAM AIRPORT SCHIPHOL
Amsterdam, The Netherlands

1. 西ターミナルから見たスキポールプラザの芝生の大屋根と管制塔
2. 中央ターミナル前面に設けられたスキポールプラザ外観
3. 西ターミナルの屋上越しに見た手前のピアFと向こう側の新設されたピアG
1. View of the Schiphol plaza's lawn roof and the control tower from the lounge west
2. View of the Schiphol plaza's facade from the roadside
3. View of the pier F and G from the lounge west

1

4. 西ターミナル2階の「フードバー・ノーチラス」からエアサイドの旅客機を見る　　4. View of an airliner from the Food Bar NAUTILUS (2F) in the lounge west

5

5.　西ターミナル1階のチケットカウンター
6.　西ターミナルのピアG内部コンコース。天井部分にはアートワークが施されている
7.　鉄道駅と一体化したスキポールプラザの入り口ホール。地下が鉄道駅となっている
5.　View of the ticket counter(1F) on the lounge west
6.　The moving sidewalks of the concourse(2F) on the pier G
7.　View of the entrance hall on the Schiphol plaza

14

6

9

10

8. 西ターミナル中3階の「ブラッセリー・ラ フォーレ」内部客席。
   設計はイギリスの建築家ナイジェル・コーツ
9. スキポールプラザ中央に配されたミーティングポイント。
   赤と白の大柄なチェッカー模様が分かりやすい
10. 西ターミナル2階のカフェ&バー

8. View of the Brasserie LA FORET(M3F) in the lounge west
9. View of the meeting point in the Schiphol plaza
10. View of the Cafe & Bar(2F) in the lounge west

11

12

11. スキポールプラザのショッピングアーケード。36の店舗が配されている
12. 地下の鉄道駅に続くエスカレーターをスキポールプラザの入り口ホールから見る
13. 中央ターミナル2階の公営カジノ前に設けられた休憩ラウンジ。閉鎖的でありながら周囲の気配が分かるラウンジチェアのデザインがユニーク
14. 中央ターミナル2階の通路に面した公営カジノの外観

11. View of the shopping arcade in the Schiphol plaza
12. View of the escalator and entrance hall in the Schiphol plaza
13. View of the resting lounge(2F) in the lounge central
14. Facade wall of the casino(2F) in the lounge central

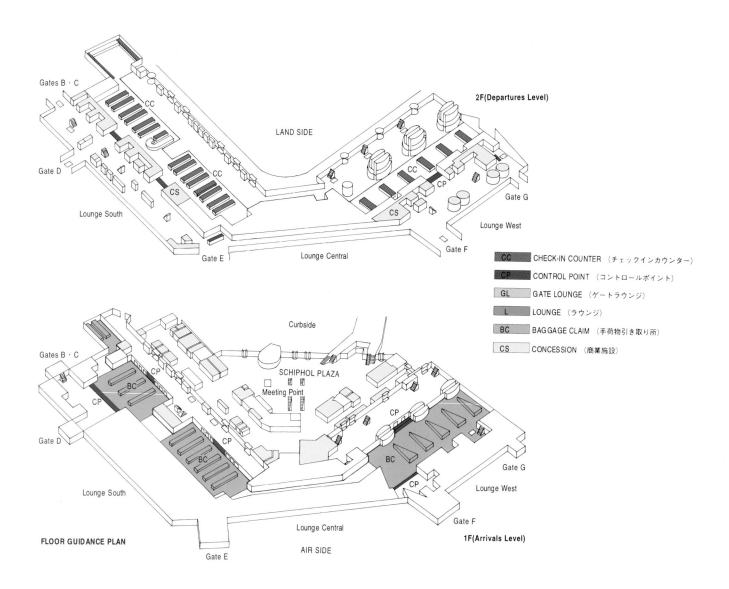

Gates B・C

CC

2F(Departures Level)

LAND SIDE

Gate D

CC

CS

Lounge South

CC

CP

Gate G

CS

Lounge West

Gate F

Gate E

Lounge Central

CC	CHECK-IN COUNTER （チェックインカウンター）
CP	CONTROL POINT （コントロールポイント）
GL	GATE LOUNGE （ゲートラウンジ）
L	LOUNGE （ラウンジ）
BC	BAGGAGE CLAIM （手荷物引き取り所）
CS	CONCESSION （商業施設）

Curbside

Gates B・C

CP

BC

CP

SCHIPHOL PLAZA

Meeting Point

CP

Gate D

CP

BC

BC

Gate G

Lounge South

CP

Lounge West

Gate F

Lounge Central

FLOOR GUIDANCE PLAN

1F(Arrivals Level)

Gate E

AIR SIDE

●世界の "ベスト・エアポート"
80社のエアラインが乗り入れ、世界90カ国、215の諸都市と結ばれているアムステルダム・スキポール空港は、1994年、利用総旅客数で2360万人を記録した。スキポール空港は、これまで度々、国際的な雑誌媒体や旅客組合などからヨーロッパのあるいは世界の "ベスト・エアポート" という評価を与えられている。また1994年度はIATA（国際航空運送協会）による大西洋横断航空旅客調査において、旅客にとっての総合的利便性という点で断トツの第1位の空港にランクされた。こうした評価は単に空港規模や旅客数といった数字だけからのものでないことは明らかであろう。ヨーロッパ内に100以上の行先を持ち、1週間の便数が2200を超えるスキポール空港はヨーロッパ有数のハブ空港としてのポジションを占めている。さらに "ワンルーフ・コンセプト"（一つ屋根の下に全ての施設があること）を大きな特徴の一つとしているスキポール空港は、ロンドンのヒースロー空港やパリのシャルルドゴール空港といった複数のターミナルを持つ空港に比べて、より明確な移動、より短い時間（正確には50分以内）に慌てずに乗り継ぎができるという乗り継ぎの簡単さとスピードの点で優位性を保っている。

●あらゆるものが揃うコンセッション＆サービス施設
中央、南、西と三つに区分された各ターミナルには、コンセッション、各種サービス施設など空港にあるべきものほとんどすべてを備えている。45のショップが揃った免税ショッピングセンターは、総販売品目は12万点を超え、このエリアは世界の "ベスト・デューティーフリー・ショッピング" に選ばれ続けている。そのほか、ターミナルホテル、授乳室、ビジネスクラス乗客用ラウンジ、ビジネスセンターなどの諸施設、ミート・アンド・アシスト・サービス、グループ会議室、身体障害者用特殊サービスなど多彩である。1993年にオープンした西ターミナルでは、これらの諸施設のほかに、イギリスの著名建築家ナイジェル・コーツの設計による豊かな飲食空間が人気を博している。また1994年には、ゴルフ練習場、日焼けサロン、フィットネスセンター、サウナなどを備えたレジャー施設が、1995年には "エアポート・カジノ" が加わり、トランジット客の空港での時間の使い方にさらに多くの選択肢が加わった。

●スキポールプラザ
1995年5月には、エアポート・ターミナルの入り口に新たにスキポールプラザがオープンした。複合ショッピングセンターとオランダ国鉄スキポール空港駅を組み込んだプラザは、コンコースをもった大きなセントラルホールであり、将来的には年間1500万人の入場者が予想されている。36の店舗や飲食施設が入ったプラザはさまざまなターゲット・グループを狙い

としており、さらに新しくオープンする予定のシェラトンホテル（1997年）およびワールドトレードセンター（1996年）とも接続する予定である。
スキポール・プラザは、地階のオランダ国鉄スキポール駅に直結しており、18分でアムステルダムの中心街に着く列車が15分おきに発車している。また、オランダ国内の各都市やドイツ、フランス、ベルギーの主要都市へも直通または1回の乗り換えで行くことができる。さらに、1998〜99年以降スキポール駅は拡張され、ヨーロッパ高速鉄道システム（TGV）が加わり、ヨーロッパの各都市までの時間が現行のほぼ半分になる予定である。

●将来計画のコンセプト
将来の需要を満たし、ワールド・ベスト・エアポートの位置を保つため、大規模な将来計画を持っている。この計画コンセプトは、十分なキャパシティの確保、ワンルーフ・コンセプトの維持、乗客およびカーゴ設備の拡張、ハイレベルなサービスの提供の四つの項目となっている。

15. スキポールプラザのカーブサイドに突き出したフォルムを持つ「サンドイッチ・デリフランス」
15. View of the Sandwiches DELIFRANCE in front of Schiphol plaza

15

● WORLD'S BEST AIRPORT

Amsterdam Airport Schiphol—from which 80 airlines provide service to 215 cities in 90 countries—served 23.6 million passengers in1994.

Schiphol has been named "best airport of the world" or "best airport of Europe" repeatedly by international magazines around the world and by passenger associations.
The most recent honor came in 1994, when Schiphol was ranked the number one airport— by a wide margin—for overall passenger convenience in a survey of transatlantic air passengers conducted by the International Air Transport Association (IATA). Schiphol is obviously a world-class airport by standards other than mere size or number of passengers served.

● HIGH LEVEL OF SERVICE

With more than 100 destinations and more than 2,200 weekly flights within Europe, Schiphol has a strong position as a European hub. Furthermore, with its "One Roof Concept," Schiphol's single terminal design is a major advantage for passengers. It allows them to make connections within 50 minutes— less time and less hassle than that required multi-terminal airports such as London's

Heathrow or Paris' Charles de Gaulle.

● COMPREHENSIVE CONCESSION AND
  SERVICE FACILITIES

The terminal's three sections—center, south and west—offer passengers almost every conceivable service. The complex has an exclusive tax-free shopping center, with 45 shops selling more than 120,000 items. This shopping center has consistently been voted the world's best duty-free shopping location. The terminal includes a hotel, rooms for nursing mothers, waiting rooms for business class passengers, a business center with relevant facilities, a meet-and-assist service, group meeting rooms and special services for the disabled. In the west part of the terminal which opened in 1993, the elegant dining area designed by Nigel Coates, a prominent English architect, is winning popularity.

● SCHIPHOL PLAZA

In May 1995, Schiphol Plaza was officially opened at the entrance of the airport terminal. The plaza, featuring a magnificent shopping complex and the Schiphol airport station of Holland National Railways, includes a large central hall. 15 million visitors per year are expected. With 36 shops and catering outlets, Schiphol Plaza will attract a variety of

customers. It will also boast a Sheraton Hotel, to be opened in 1997, and a World Trade Center to be opened in 1996.

Trains leave Schiphol Plaza for downtown Amsterdam every 15 minutes. The trip takes only 18 minutes. Passengers can travel to other Dutch cities or to those of Germany, France and Belgium directly or with one transfer. Beginning in 1998 or 1999, Schiphol will be connected to the European High Speed Rail System (TGV), which means that transit time to other European destinations will be shortened by half.

● PLANNING FOR THE FUTURE

To meet future demand and to maintain its position as one of the "best airports in the world," Schiphol is conducting a massive renovation and expansion program. The program's four goals are:
- Securing sufficient capacity
- Maintaining the one roof concept
- Enhancing passenger and cargo facilities
- Providing a high level of service

Text and Data Contributor
Terminal Marketing & communications
Amsterdam Airport Schiphol

ヨーロッパの地理的中心を占める有利さときめ細かいサービスで急成長

ウィーン国際空港

オーストリア，ウィーン

VIENNA INTERNATIONAL AIRPORT

A-8000 Wien-Flughafen, Austria

1. 到着フロアである1階の中央部を占めるバゲージクレーム（手荷物引き取り所）。
   天井のルーバーから自然光が降り注ぐ明るい空間構成となっている
2. ターミナル中央のタワー状に張り出した建築部分外観をエアサイドから見る
3. 古都・ウィーンらしい伝統的な意匠を高窓に採り入れたターミナル2階のホールとそれに続くチケットカウンター
1. View of the baggage claim(1F)
2. View of the terminal from the air side
3. View of the ticket counter(2F)

1

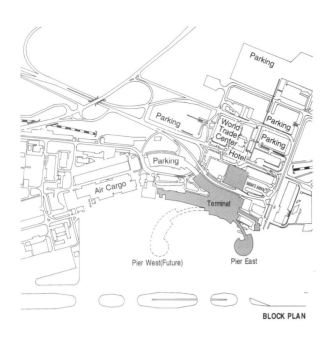

BLOCK PLAN

4

5

4. ターミナル2階から駐車場へ至る通路両側に設けられたショッピングアーケード。天井から吊り下げられたドライフラワーをトップライトが活き活きと見せている
5. ターミナル2階中央のショッピングプラザ。34のショップがテナントとして入居している
6. 東側ピアの中央広場と待合ロビー。ここにも自然光が採り入れられている
7. 東側ピアのボーディング・ラウンジを通路から見る

4. View of the shopping arcade(2F)
5. View of the center hall in the shopping plaza(2F)
6. View of the hall and waiting lobby in the east pier
7. View of the boarding lounge and passage in the east pier

6

7

8

9

10

11

8. ターミナル3階レストランフロアに至るアプローチ
   通路に設けられたトップライトを持つ吹き抜け
9. 10. ターミナル3階にあるエグゼクティブ・ラウンジ。
   ゆったりとしたゴージャスな雰囲気である
11. ターミナル3階の最奥にある「レストラン・ル グルメ」
   内部客席
8. View of the top lighting and corridor(3F)
9. 10. Interior view of the executive lounge(3F)
11. Interior view of the restaurant
   Le Gourme(3F)

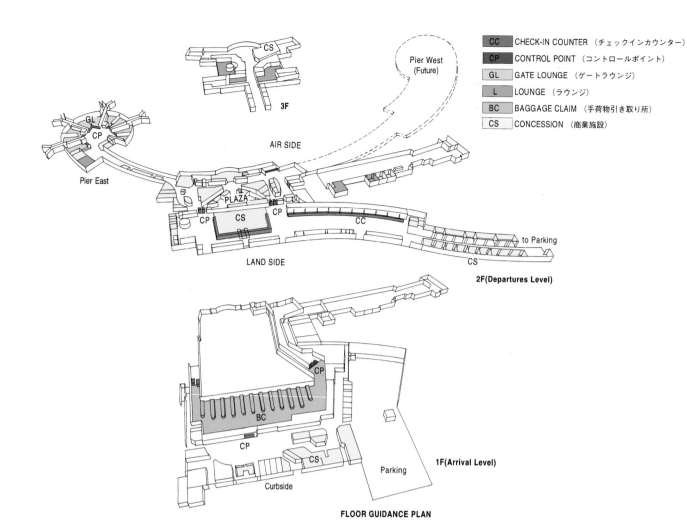

Pier West (Future)

3F

AIR SIDE

GL
CP

Pier East

PLAZA

CP
CS
CP
CC

to Parking

CS

LAND SIDE

2F(Departures Level)

CP

BC

CP

CS

Parking

1F(Arrival Level)

Curbside

FLOOR GUIDANCE PLAN

●東欧諸国の自由化とともに，新たな発展を遂げる西欧圏と東欧圏の接点であるウィーン空港は，1980年代末の東欧諸国の自由化とともに，新しい時代を迎えたと言えよう。西ヨーロッパ最東に位置していたこの空港が，ＥＵによる新体制のヨーロッパでは，地理的にその中心的位置を占めるようになり，広く東欧近隣諸国やアジアの旅客に対して魅力あるサービスを提供するウィーン国際空港へと発展を遂げている。

ウィーン市街の中心から南東約16kmに位置するこの空港は，第２次大戦後，英国空軍の管理下にあったが，1954年から国と州と市の出資によるウィーン航空公団が管理・運営を引き継ぎ，商業空港としてスタートを切った。1982年には，空港から数百メートル離れたところにある高速道路が，ハンガリー，スロバキア，チェコを通過するヨーロッパ高速道路網と連結し，ヨーロッパにおけるウィーン国際空港の重要性が増大する。その間，継続的な航空需要の増加に伴い，施設的には1977年に第２滑走路が建設され，さらに1988年には八つのボーディングブリッジを持つ東ピアが新設された。このピアは，音楽の都ウィーンらしく，バイオリンの先端のスクロール（糸蔵の渦巻き装飾）をイメージしてデザインされている。1990年から2000年の10年間に航空需要は２倍に

なるという予測のもと，1989年からはさらに大規模な拡張工事が始まっている。1996年に予定されている12のブリッジを持つ西ピアの開設をもって，拡張工事は一応完了する予定である。

●空港規模に見合ったきめの細かい旅客サービス
ウィーン市街までのアクセスは，ターミナル地階に発着する鉄道で約35分，高速道路を利用して車で約15分，市中のヒルトンホテルに併設されているシティ・エア・ターミナルまで24時間運行されている直通バスで20〜30分である。
空港ターミナルビルには，アーケードとプラザという二つのショッピングエリアがあり，計53の専門店および免税店が入居している。
1995年にはこのラインアップにハロッズ・デパートも加わり，年間770万人を数える旅客にスワロフスキーのクリスタルやデーメルのお菓子といったオーストリアの有名商品だけでなく，インターナショナルな商品構成によるショッピングを提供している。飲食部門では，14のレストラン，スナックバーがあり，ファストフードから高級グルメ料理までさまざまな食事を楽しむことができる。
このほか，ウィーン空港では，
・東西ヨーロッパを結ぶ大規模な空路網によるゲー

トウエーとトランスファー機能の充実。
・東南アジアおよび日本からの旅行者にとっての新ヨーロッパへの玄関口として，西欧基準での顧客サービスの提供。
・子供たちのためのプレイルームや保育室，ハンディキャップのある旅客のための施設の充実。ビジネス客が出発前の静かなひとときを過ごすことができる８カ所のビジネスラウンジ，ＶＩＰルームやビジネス・センターの完備。24時間体制の医療設備。といった多様なプログラムにより，空港のサービス機能の向上に努めている。新ヨーロッパにおける位置的有利性を背景に，ヨーロッパで最も急成長を遂げている空港の一つであるウィーン国際空港は，空港規模に見合ったきめの細かい顧客サービスという面でも急成長を遂げている。

12. 音楽の都・ウィーンにふさわしくバイオリンのスクロール（弦柱頭）をかたどった東側ピアのフォルムが分かる空撮ショット
13. 上空から見たターミナル全景。角翼型のピア配置を採用している
12. Bird's-eye view of the east pier (Photo credit／VIA)
13. Full shot of the terminal building from the air (Photo credit／VIA)

12

13

●PROGRESS ACHIEVED THROUGH LIB-ERATION OF THE NATIONS OF EASTERN EUROPE

Vienna International Airport, located where Western Europe meets Eastern Europe, entered a new era when the borders to the former Eastern bloc opened at the end of the 1980s. The easternmost airport in Western Europe became a centrally located airport in the new Europe. Vienna International Airport now offers attractive services for passengers from Eastern and Western Europe, Asia and the rest of the globe.

The airport, located 16 kilometers southeast of downtown Vienna, began service as a commercial airport in 1954. The Vienna Aviation Authority, with financial support from the national, regional and city government, assumed management responsibility from the Royal Air Force. In 1982, the Eastern Motorway, which passes within a few hundred meters of the airport, was linked with the European motorway network passing through Hungary, Slovakia and the Czech Republic. Thus, Vienna International Airport's importance in Europe was enhanced. Due to continually increasing traffic, a second

runway was built in 1977, and a pier with 8 boarding bridges in 1988. This pier is designed in the shape of a violin's scroll to represent Vienna, the city of music. In anticipation of a doubling of passenger volume in the 1990s, a further large-scale expansion was started in 1989. The 1996 opening of the new Pier West with 12 bridges will complete this expansion program.

●SOPHISTICATED CUSTOMER SERVICES APPROPRIATE FOR PASSENGER VOLUME

One can travel from the airport to downtown Vienna by car in about 15 minutes, using the expressway, or by train in about 35 minutes. The train station is under the airport. Busses run between the airport and the city air terminal located in the mid-city Hilton Hotel around the clock, taking 20 to 30minutes.

Two shopping areas in the terminal building, named "Arcade" and "Plaza," accommo-date 53 regular and duty free shops. In 1995, Harrod's opened a store in the complex. The shops offer not only Austrian merchandise, such as Swalovsky's crystal and sweets from Demel, but also goods from around the world. 14 restaurants and snack bars offer every kind

of dining—from fast food to elegant cuisines.

Vienna Airport endeavors to improve its services by providing a great diversity of programs such as:

- Improved gateway and transfer systems for an extensive air network between Eastern and Western Europe.
- Western style customer services at a key entry-point to the new Europe
- A children's playground and a nursery room, barrier-free facility for the disabled, eight business lounges where business travellers can relax before departure, a VIP room, a business center and around -the-clock medical care.

With its prime location in the new Europe, Vienna International Airport has become one of the fastest-growing airports in the region. The airport has improved its customer services in a manner that is appropriate for its passenger volume.

Text and Data Contributor
Hans Mayer : Public Relations
Vienna International Airport

ランドスケープとテクノスケープとの巧みな融合

ミュンヘン空港

ドイツ, バイエルン州, ミュンヘン

MÜNCHEN AIRPORT
München,Bavaria,Germany

1. エアサイドから長さ約1kmにおよぶターミナルビルと高さ78mの管制塔をみる
2. 道路越しにターミナルB・C間のカーブサイドを見る。セントラル・エリアへと続く地下通路から明かりが洩れる
3. ターミナルBのガラスアトリウム開口部を外部から見る
1. View of the terminal from the air side
2. Night view of curbside of the terminal from the central area
3. View of the terminal B

1

4. セントラル・エリアのメーンホール。エスカレーターは地下の鉄道駅へと繋がる
5. 出発ラウンジに設置されたエレベーター
6. 出発ラウンジを2Fレベルから見下ろす。高い天井とガラス開口部採用によって明るく快適な空間を創り出す
4. View of the main hall and escalators (to rapid transit trains) in the central area
5. View of a glass elevator at the departure lounge
6. View of departure lounge from the second floor

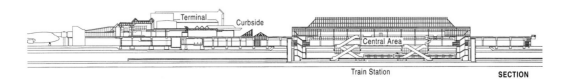

SECTION

5

6

4

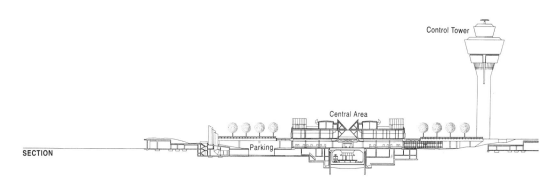

Control Tower

Central Area

SECTION

Parking

7

8

7. ターミナルビルの地下1階には動く歩道（エスカレーター）が張り巡らされ、AからEまでの各ターミナル間のほか、ホテルやビジネスセンターへのアクセスも容易にしている
8. 空港敷地内にある「ディスコクラブ・ナイトフライト」。周辺にはビジターズ・パーク（空港を訪れる観光客向けの公園）やカーゴ・ターミナルなどが点在している
9. 幅1.4mのこの動く歩道は、ターミナルビル内のすべてを合わせると全長2.7kmにもおよぶ
10. 「ナイトフライト」店内。若い世代に人気を博しているナイトスポット

7. The moving sidewalks of the terminal
8. Entry of the Disco NIGHT FLIGHT
9. The moving sidewalks.Their total length is over 2,700m
10. Interior view of the Disco NIGHT FLIGHT

9

10

13

14

11、12. セントラル・エリア地下1階レベルのカフェから吹き抜け空間を飾るインスタレーションを見る。セントラル・エリアは総床面積4万6000m²、27のチェックインカウンターや各種サービスデスク、商業施設などが集積しており、ミュンヘン空港の賑わいの中心となっている

13. ターミナルBにあるイタリアンレストラン上部に吊られた照明オブジェ。作者はドイツの照明デザイナー、インゴ・マウラー

14. ターミナルBにあるダイクロイックガラスを用いたオブジェ。作者はアメリカのガラスアーチスト、ジェームス・カーペンター

15. 空港に隣接する「ホテル・ケンピンスキー」の中央吹き抜け空間を見下ろす

11、12. View of the cafe and art objects in the central area

13. View of the art objects in Italian restaurant in the terminal B

14. View of the art objects in the terminal B

15. View of the Hotel KEMPINSKI from outside

15

16

17

●人々を魅了する「テクノスケープ（技術景観）」
1992年5月17日にオープンしたミュンヘン空港は、人々を魅了する大きなパワーを持っている。その年には170万人もの観光客が訪れ、有名なお伽話の城「ノイシュバンシュタイン（Neuschwanstein）」を押しのけ、バイエルン地方の観光アトラクションとして最大の訪問客数を記録した。
ミュンヘン空港は、多くの構造物と機能エリアを備えているが、全体としての設備は"調和のとれた集合体"という特徴がある。そのため、多様性の中にも明確な統一性がある。個々の建築物だけでなく、全体としての施設は空間がゆったりとしていて、半透明で明るい。目に見えるデザインの中には高いレベルの恒久性があり、他とは異なる個性を持つ。高い技術的レベルとローカルでヒューマンな安定感の両方を具現化した、未来都市を予見させる個性を持っている。2000年には利用客数は2000万人になると見込まれている。長さ4000m、幅60mという二つの滑走路は2300m離れて設置されており、毎時90機の離着陸のキャパシティを持ち、年間約20万機の離着陸をさばいている。

●乗客の快適性を考えた設計
年間1800～2000万人の乗客を処理できるよう設計された「ターミナルビル」は、五つの到着エリアと四つの出発エリアからなるモジュラー設計で、乗客の快

適さと特徴的な透明空間とを統合した巨大な複合建築である。乗客の移動は「セントラルビル」の設置で、より明解になり、かつ多様なニーズに応えている。出発ゲートからワンフロア下に降りると動く歩道があり、乗客、出迎えの人、そして他のビジターはターミナルの一方の端から反対側まで迅速に進むことができる。また、低層に広がるターミナルは「到着」と「出発」が交互に並んでいるため、実際、利用客が歩く距離が少なくて済む。「セントラルビル」はターミナルに直接隣接していて、空港利用者はここにあるレストラン、ショップ、チェックイン＆インフォメーションデスクなどを利用することができる。また高速輸送鉄道駅もあり、およそ30～35分でミュンヘン中心部に行くことができる。1997年には空港に通じる鉄道がもう1本開通する予定である。車による空港利用者は、アウトバーン出口を出て広い2車線の高速道路に入れば空港に直接入ることができる。ターミナルのすぐ隣には、地下式駐車場4棟と多層式駐車場3棟の合計1万台用の駐車スペースがある。

●エコロジカルなランドスケープ
空港建設に関しては、周辺環境との協調が大きな課題であった。特に騒音防止、廃棄物管理、エネルギー供給、生態面での環境協調などさまざまな問題を考慮しながら進められた。建築家、景観プランナー、そしてデザイナーは新しい設備の外観が周囲の田舎

の景観とできるだけ調和するように努めた。空港が建設されたエルディンガームース(Erdinger Moos)固有の景観の特徴を採り入れ、空港は環境の一部であるとの認識にたち、建設計画が行われた。この土地の特徴である平坦さ、真っ直ぐな道路、整然とまとまった緑樹の区域が、ユニークで特徴的な"空港景観"デザインの要素となっている。建築物の高さ制限、および緑樹までの距離を最大に取ることなどが空港をその周囲にうまく溶け込ませるための重要な要素であった。

16. 左手のカーブサイドと駐車場に挟まれてA92号線へ続く道路が走る。ランドサイドには意識的に多くのグリーンが配されている
17. 空港駅の隣駅「ビジターズ・パーク」と公園を結ぶガラス張りのチューブトンネル
16. View of the landside
17. View of the rapid transit train stop "Visitors' Park"

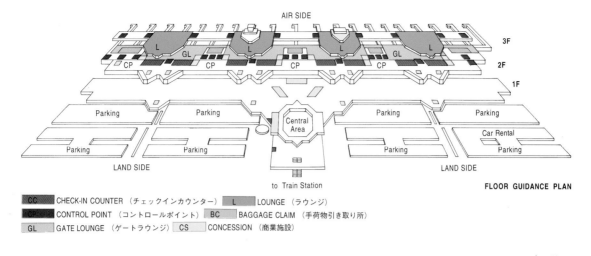

AIR SIDE

3F
2F
1F

L · GL · CP · L · CP · L · CP · L · GL · CP · L

Parking · Parking · Central Area · Parking · Parking

Car Rental
Parking

Parking · Parking · Parking

LAND SIDE · LAND SIDE

to Train Station

FLOOR GUIDANCE PLAN

CC CHECK-IN COUNTER （チェックインカウンター）　L LOUNGE （ラウンジ）
CP CONTROL POINT （コントロールポイント）　BC BAGGAGE CLAIM （手荷物引き取り所）
GL GATE LOUNGE （ゲートラウンジ）　CS CONCESSION （商業施設）

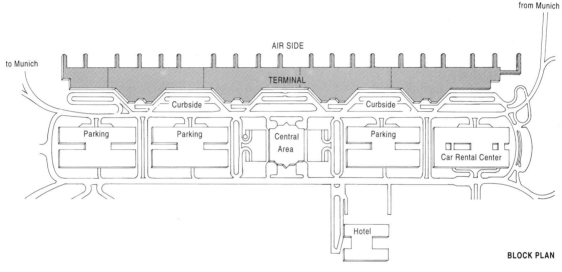

from Munich

AIR SIDE

to Munich

TERMINAL

Curbside · Curbside

Parking · Parking · Central Area · Parking · Car Rental Center

Hotel

BLOCK PLAN

● "TECHNOSCAPE" FASCINATES VISITORS
Munich Airport, opened on May 17th, 1992, has a great power to fascinate, judging by its vast numbers of visitors. In its inaugural year, the new airport attracted 1.7 million, nosing past Neuschwanstein, the famous fairly-tale castle, to become the biggest hit among Bavaria's tourist attractions.

Although Munich Airport features a large number of different structures and functional areas, the facility as a whole has the character of a harmonious ensemble. The variety includes a certain visual unity. Not just isolated structures, but the complex as a whole is spacious, lucent and bright. The cohesion of visual design gives Munich Airport a distinct identity that expresses not only its aspiration to the high technological standards of the future city but also its aim to blend harmoniously with the surrounding countryside and residents.

It is estimated that 20 million passengers will use the complex in the year 2000. The airport's two runways, each 4,000 meters long and 60 meters wide and built 2,300 meters apart, have the capacity to handle up to 90 aircraft movements an hour. Some 200,000 aircraft take off and land each year.

● DESIGNED FOR A HIGH DEGREE OF PASSENGER COMFORT
The terminal building, designed to deal with up to 18～20 million passengers a year, is a megacomplex that combines a distinctive, translucent space with a high degree of passenger comfort. It features a modular design comprising five arrival and four departure areas. The Central Building makes passenger movement easier and provides a variety of goods and services. One floor down from the departure and arrival gates, moving walkways allow passengers and other visitors to proceed quickly and conveniently from one end of the terminal to the other. Because the arrival and departure areas are arranged in alternating order, the low and wide terminal building shortens the passenger's walking distance.

The Central Building adjoins the terminal. Here the airport users find restaurants, shops, check-in and information desks, etc . A rapid transit railway provides transportation to downtown Munich in about 30～35 minutes. A second railway line to the airport will open in 1997. Those travelling to the airport by car enjoy a separate autobahn exit and a broad, high-speed dual carriageway that takes them straight into the airport. The airport provides a

total of 10,000 parking spaces in four underground and three multi-story car parks next to the terminal.

● ENVIRONMENT-FRIENDLY DESIGN
In consideration of the surrounding region, the airport's development included such considerations as noise reduction, waste management, and energy supply. The architects, landscape planners and designers took steps to ensure that the appearance of the new facilities harmonized with the surrounding countryside. Erdinger Moos, where the airport was built, is primarily agricultural, so efforts were made to construct an airport that adopted the existing local sensibilities and reflected the colors and forms of the local landscape. The land's characteristics—its flatness, its straight lines and its neatly grouped areas of greenery—became elements in the design of a unique and distinct "airport landscape". The restraint exercised in the height of structures, and the devotion of a maximum of space to greenery, were key factors in the successful integration of the airport into its setting.

Text and Data Contributor
Hans-Joachim Bues
Press Department
Munich Airport

巨大な空港を支える効率性とサービスの快適性

シンガポール・チャンギ空港

シンガポール，チャンギ

SINGAPORE CHANGI AIRPORT
Changi,Singapore

1. 管制塔とターミナル1の外観を見る。
   花と緑に囲まれた広大な敷地の大半は埋め立て地である
2. 南国らしくパーキングスペースも緑陰の下になるように計画されている
3. 広々としたターミナル2のカーブサイド夜景。左端に見えるのは管制塔
1. View of the control tower and terminal 1 from the site
2. View of the parking area under the shade of trees
3. Night view of the curbside in front of terminal 2

1

4

5

4. ターミナル1の2階・出発チェックインホールと窓外に広がるグリーンを3階から見る
5. 効果的にグリーンを配したターミナル2の2階出発ロビーから1階到着ロビーに至る階段とエスカレーターまわり
6. ターミナル2の2階出発ロビー。右側はチェックインカウンター
4. View of the departure hall(2F) in the terminal 1
5. View of the stair and escalator from the second floor to the first floor in the terminal 2
6. View of the departure hall and ticket counter(2F) in the terminal 2

7．ターミナル1の3階から見た2階出発ホール。チェックインなどの手続きがスムーズに進むよう通路やカウンターなども余裕のある面積がとられている

7. View of the departure hall(2F) on the terminal 1

8. ターミナル2の2階トランジットエリアに配された
   シンガポールのシティインフォメーションコーナー
9. ターミナル1のエアサイドに面した2階出発ロビー
   の待合ラウンジ。いたるところにグリーンや生花
   がディスプレイされ、旅行客を迎える
10. ターミナル1の3階にあるエグゼクティブ・ラウンジ
    内部を見る
11. ターミナル2の3階トランジットホテル受付カウン
    ターまわり

8. View of the information center(2F) in the
   terminal 2
9. View of the waiting lobby(2F) in the
   terminal 1
10. Interior view of the executive lounge(3F)
    in the terminal 1
11. View of the transit hotel's reception(3F)
    in the terminal 2

11

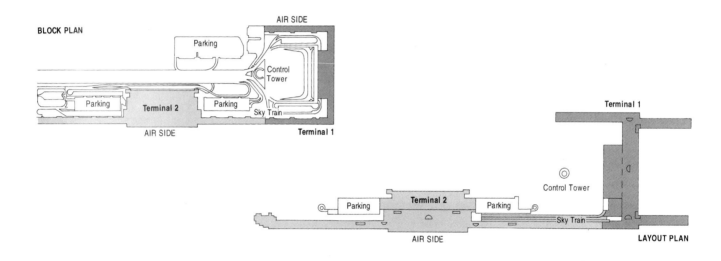

● 貿易立国シンガポールの表玄関

東南アジアの海路の要衝に位置するという地の利を生かして、シンガポールは1965年の建国以来、貿易立国を国策として目覚ましい発展を遂げてきた。そして今や東南アジアだけでなく、世界の貿易における中継基地としての地歩を固めている。このシンガポールの表玄関として機能しているのが、南シナ海に面した島の東端に建設されたチャンギ空港である。人口約260万人、600km²という狭い国土に比較して巨大なスケールを持つ空港は、敷地の半分以上が海を埋め立てたものであり、1975年に建設が始まり、1981年に完成した。

現在では、トランジット(乗り換え)の客を含め年間旅客量は3500万人に達し、アジア太平洋地区では最大を誇っている。さらに増加する航空量に対応するため、21世紀初頭に完成予定の第三のターミナルの建設が計画されるなど、旅客に快適性と利便性を供給する理念と需要に一歩先んじたキャパシティ維持により、21世紀にむけて大きな成長を目指している。

● 世界で有数のハブ空港

空港運営の基本的な理念は、"シンガポールの発展は世界との密接な連携なくしてはあり得ない"ということであり、国際線のゲートウエーとしてトップの座を占めるようになったのも、この考えに基づき空港

を世界に向けて自由化したためであろう。多くのエアラインを招き、広く世界の目的地とを繋げる「空の開放」政策はシンガポールの国策でもあり、この結果、チャンギ空港は67社の国際エアラインにより54カ国、128都市と連結されている。

シンガポールの中心街より車で約20分の位置にある空港のメーンの施設は二つのターミナルであるが、その最大の特徴は十分な広さと快適性にある。到着ロビーや出発ロビー、それらをつなぐ通路などパブリックな空間は広々として混雑や渋滞とは無縁であり、しかも機能的に構成されているので利用客はゆったりとした気分で施設を利用できる。これらのパブリックな空間は「クリーン&グリーン」を目標とし、切り花による生花がふんだんにディスプレイされ、待合ロビーの池や泉とともに南国らしさを演出し、清潔で緑あふれる空港としてのホスピタリティーを表現している。

● ミニ都市としての都市機能の充実

世界各国の旅行雑誌のセレクションで、その効率性と旅行者の快適さを実現するための行き届いたサービスにより、常に上位に選出されているチャンギ空港の売り物は、ミニ都市と言われている多様な商業とサービス施設の集積である。ターミナル1とターミナル2を合わせて103の小売店があり、旅行客が買い

たいと思うあらゆる商品が品揃えされている。シンガポールは酒、タバコ類を除いて事実上、免税国家であり、高価なファッション・ブランド品から電子工業製品、菓子類からおもちゃにいたるまでの商品が市内の商店街と同じ値段で買えるのである。

つまり、買い物に関しては大規模なショッピングセンターを空港が併設しているのと同じことであり、商品の安さを保障するためにCAAS(シンガポール航空公団)は常に小売店の価格をチェックし、市内と同じレベルに保っている。

また、小売店以外にもレストラン21店、ビジネスセンターを持つトランジット・ホテルが二つ、フィットネスセンター、プール、プレイエリアなど、乗り換え客が楽しく時間を過ごせるようミニ都市並みの施設が用意されている。

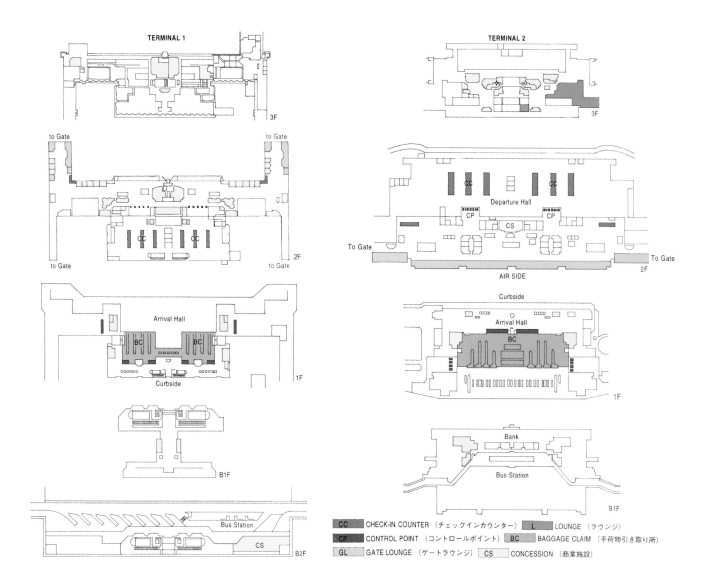

TERMINAL 1

3F

to Gate   to Gate

to Gate   to Gate
CC   CC
2F

Arrival Hall
BC   BC
Curbside
1F

B1F

Bus Station
CS
B2F

TERMINAL 2

3F

Departure Hall
CC   CC
CP   CP
CS
To Gate   To Gate
2F
AIR SIDE

Curbside
Arrival Hall
BC
1F

Bank

Bus Station
B1F

CC	CHECK-IN COUNTER （チェックインカウンター）	L	LOUNGE （ラウンジ）
CP	CONTROL POINT （コントロールポイント）	BC	BAGGAGE CLAIM （手荷物引き取り所）
GL	GATE LOUNGE （ゲートラウンジ）	CS	CONCESSION （商業施設）

● THE FRONT DOOR OF SINGAPORE, A NATION OF TRADERS

Ideally situated at the center of Southeast Asian cargo routes, Singapore has achieved remarkable development since its independence in 1965 and the subsequent national policy promoting the country as a nation of traders. Today the country holds a firm position as a key hub of world trade.

Changi Airport, which serves as the "front door" of Singapore, is constructed at the east end of the island, facing the South China Sea.

The airport is enormous for a country with only 600 square kilometers of land and a population of 2.6 million. More than half of the airport is built on land reclaimed from the sea. Construction began in 1975 and was completed in 1981.

Changi Airport can handle 35 million passengers per year, the largest capacity of any airport in the Asia-Pacific region. While adhering to the goal of creating comfort and convenience for visitors, airport management is planning development to keep capacity a step ahead of demand. Terminal 3 is slated for completion early next century.

● LEADING HUB AIRPORT IN THE WORLD

Crucial to Singapore's growth has been her connection to the world. The country's emergence as a top international gateway owes much to its "open sky" policy, which is aimed at getting as many airlines to fly here—and linking the island to many destinations worldwide—as possible. The airport is served by 67 international airlines flying to 128 cities in 54 countries.

The airport's two terminals, located 20 minutes by car from the downtown area, feature extensive space and a high level of comfort. The huge space devoted to arrival and departure halls and other passageways completely eliminates congestion, and the functional design ensures that passengers and other visitors can use the facility in a very relaxed manner. The airport expresses its hospitality by displaying plenty of fresh flowers, and by the inclusion of ponds or fountains at waiting halls. These touches create an atmosphere of a clean, green and spacious tropical country.

● MERCHANDISE THE SAME PRICE AS DOWNTOWN'S

Changi Airport has been continuously selected

by publications around the world as a "World's Leading Airport" for its efficiency and detailed attention to visitor's comfort. It resembles a mini-city, with 100 shops in Terminals 1 and 2. Visitors can find a variety of competitively-priced goods because, with the exception of liquor, cigarettes and tobacco, goods sold in transit is tax-free. Thus, merchandise ranging from fashionable brands, electronic goods and confectionary to toys, etc., are available at prices the same as those downtown. The facility is like a huge shopping center, and the Civil Aviation Authority of Singapore (CAAS) monitors prices to ensure competitiveness.

Aside from the shops, a host of other facilities are available at Changi Airport for those with time to spend. The 21 restaurants, two hotels with business and fitness centers, a swimming pool and jacuzzi, the play area and other facilities contribute to the mini-city atmosphere.

Text and Data Contributor
Michelle Tay
Public Relations Officer
Singapore Changi Airport

ロッキー山脈をイメージしたシンボリックな巨大空港

デンバー国際空港

アメリカ, コロラド州, デンバー

DENVER INTERNATIONAL AIRPORT

Denver, Colorado, USA

1

1. 雪を頂いたロッキーの山並みを背後にテント膜構造の特徴のあるシルエットを浮かび上がらせた東側外観夕景。建築のフォルムはロッキー山脈をモチーフとしている
1. Sunset view of the terminal buildings from the east

2

3

2. テント膜のキャノピーが張り出した西側カーブサイドを見る
3. 東側から見たターミナル全景。草原に忽然と出現する姿が印象的
4. メーンターミナルとそこへ至るアプローチ道路を南側から見る
5. エアサイドから見たターミナル。中央のブリッジはメーンターミナルとコンコースAを結んでおり、その下をジェット機が通り抜けられる高さを持っている

2. View of the west curbside from the north
3. Full view of the terminal buildings from the east
4. View of the approach road and terminal buildings from the south
5. View of the passenger bridge from the air side

4

5

7

8

6. メーンターミナルの2階から吹き抜けを通して見た1階中央のグレートホール全景。テント膜特有の柔らかな自然光が巨大な空間を満たしている
7. コンコースBの1階中央吹き抜けとアートワーク。制作はアリス・アダムス
8. メーンターミナル1階からコンコースAの2階へ至る旅客者用ブリッジの動く歩道
9. コンコースAの中央吹き抜けとトランスポーテーションをテーマとした環境インスタレーションを2階から見る

6. Full view of the great hall(2F) in the main terminal
7. View of the hall(1F) and art works in the concourse B
8. View of the passenger bridge from the main terminal to the concourse A
9. View of the hall and art installations in the concourse A

10

11

10. コンコースCの吹き抜けとインテリアガーデン。グリーンと一体化したアート作品の制作はミカエル・シンガー

11. コンコースAの2階にあるエグゼクティブ・ラウンジ内部。中央吹き抜けを見下ろす位置にある

12. メーンターミナルの2階チケット＆チェックイン・カウンターまわり。ステンレスを多用したクールなデザインを採用している

13. メーンターミナルの2階北端から旅客者用ブリッジ越しにコンコースA方向を見る

10. View of the center hall(1F) and interior garden in the concourse C

11. Interior view of the executive lounge(2F) in the concourse A

12. View of the ticket counter(2F) in the main terminal

13. View from the main terminal(2F) to the concourse A

12

13

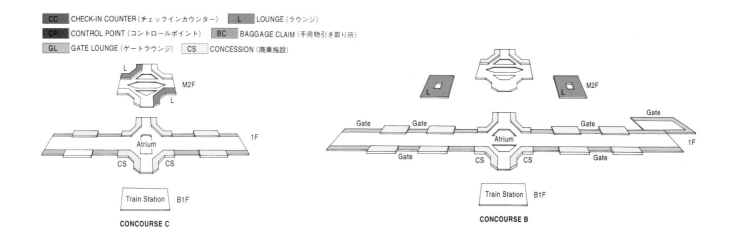

L

M2F

L

1F

Atrium

CS   CS

Train Station   B1F

CONCOURSE C

L

M2F   L

Gate   Gate   Gate   Gate

Atrium   1F

Gate   CS   CS   Gate

Train Station   B1F

CONCOURSE B

●生まれ変わった世界有数のメガ空港
1995年2月28日，世界でも有数の巨大空港デンバー国際空港がついに開港した。アメリカのほぼ中央に位置するデンバーは，地理的にも全米航空路線網の上でも重要な拠点である。1970年代中期にはデンバー市および郡当局により，将来的な航空需要の増大を見越し，既存のステイプルトン空港の大規模な拡張もしくは新空港建設が必要であるとの決定が下された。最終的には1989年5月に，ステイプルトン空港の北東（デンバー市内から約40km）に新空港の建設が行われることが住民投票により可決され，同年11月に着工された。
その後，5年半の歳月を経て，総工費42億ドル（約4200億円），総敷地面積1万1760ha（ニューヨーク・マンハッタン島の約2倍）の威容を誇るメガ空港の完成を見ることとなった。現行の施設はゲート数84，3650mの滑走路5本を有し，初年度3160万人の旅客に対応可能であるが，2020年までには，ゲート数260，滑走路12本，旅客数1億1000万人に対応する空前の

巨大空港となる予定である。なお，ステイプルトン空港は閉港され，ここでは教育やテクノロジー研究分野での再活用を検討する「ステイプルトン・トゥモロー・コンセプト・プラン」が進行中である。

●ロッキー山脈をイメージさせる膜屋根構造
デンバー国際空港のターミナルは，旅客のスムーズな流れと多様な利便性の提供を主な設計目的とし，またそのデザインにはローカル・アイデンティティーが高い水準で表現されている。ランドサイド側のメインターミナルとエアサイド側の3本のコンコースから構成され，それらは地下鉄（AGTS＝Automated Guideway Transit System）で結ばれている。
約14万m²の広さを持つメーンターミナルビルは，ロッキー山脈をイメージしたテフロン加工のファイバーグラス製大屋根に覆われ，日中は柔らかく影のない自然採光がアトリウムを照らす。夜間にはライトアップされた大屋根が，デンバーの壮大な建築的シンボルとして浮かび上がる。南側の大きなガラス

壁を通して，ロッキー山脈の景色を眺めることもできる。中央アトリウムには，中庭のレストランやカジュアルな飲食施設を含むさまざまなコンセッション施設が並ぶと同時に，レンタカーやRTDバスなど各交通機関のカウンター，観光インフォメーション，手荷物用ロッカー，旅行代理店などの各種サービスが集中している。
デンバー国際空港の大きな特徴の一つとして，メーンターミナル，各コンコース，地下鉄のトンネル内などパブリック・スペース各所に配されたアートワークが挙げられる。彫刻，大壁画，サボテン庭園，空港建設中に発見された化石を象眼したフロアアートなど大小全26タイトルのアートワークが旅客を楽しませてくれる。特に3本のコンコースそれぞれの中央スペースに設けられた環境アートはサインとして旅客が安心できる存在でもあり，圧巻である。

●発展するコンセッション施設
デンバー国際空港のコンセッション・プログラムは，デンバー市および郡当局が掲げるDBE（Disadvantaged Business Enterprise＝不利な条件を持つ企業）の参加促進という政策を実現しつつ，高水準のサービスと収益を達成することを目標に，旅客に対する最良の商品展示，街頭価格の保持，旅客の需要に合った商品構成およびサービスといったコンセプトで運営されている。メーンターミナル，各コンコースに設けられた1万3100m²のエリアには，飲食，サービス，リテールショップおよび免税ショップなど，100店舗を超えるコンセッション施設が営業している。また，将来的には，旅客のニーズに応じた新たな専門店街の開発のほか，フィットネス・センター，インタラクティブ機能を有する航空博物館，登山活動センターなどのプログラムも予定されている。

14

14. ポエティックな表情を見せる早朝の空港。中央の旅客者用ブリッジは右側のメーンターミナルと左側のコンコースAを結んでいる
14. Morning view of the passenger bridge from the west to the east

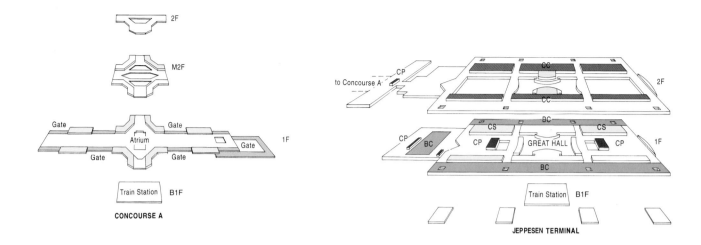

CONCOURSE A

JEPPESEN TERMINAL

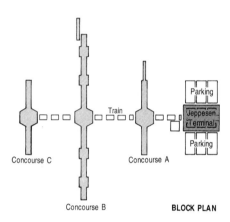

BLOCK PLAN

● WORLD'S FOREMOST MEGA AIRPORT
On February 28th, 1995, Denver International Airport was finally inaugurated as the world's foremost mega airport. Located in the center of the United States, Denver is an important base for many U.S. air routes.

In the mid-1970s, the City and the County of Denver determined that new airport facilities were necessary, and they discussed whether to augment facilities at the existing Stapleton International Airport or to construct a new airport to meet future aviation needs. In May 1989, the citizens of the city and county, in a referendum, endorsed construction of a new airport northeast of Stapleton (about 40 kilometers from Downtown Denver). Construction began in November of the same year.

After five and one-half years of construction, the mega airport was completed at a cost of $4.2 billion. Its area of 11,760 hectares is roughly double that of Manhattan Island, New York. The facility has 84 gates and five 3,650-meter runways, which can serve 31.6 million passengers per year. However by the year 2020, it will grow to an epoch-making mammoth airport—260 gates and 12 runways will accommodate up to 110 million passengers a year.

Stapleton International Airport has closed. The Stapleton Tomorrow Concept Plan, designed to make effective use of the facilities at the old airport, is now in process, emphasizing the creation opportunities through education and technology.

● MAIN TERMINAL WITH A FIBERGLASS
ROOF IN THE IMAGE OF THE ROCKIES
The primary objective for the terminal design was to create smooth traffic flow and a diversity of conveniences. The building is formed with the main terminal on the land side and three concourses on the air side. These areas are connected by the Automated Guideway Transit System. The main terminal building has approximately 140,000 square meters of floor space, and it is covered by a distinctive translucent roof of teflon-coated fiberglass designed in the image of the Rocky Mountains. Soft, shadowless natural light illuminates the atrium during the day. At night, lit from within, the roof becomes a spectacular beacon and a new architectural symbol for Denver.

Travelers have a breathtaking view of the Rocky Mountains through the massive glass wall on the south end. At the atrium, passengers find a variety of shops, restaurants including a food court and casual dining establishments. Many services are available, such as car rental, bus reservations, tourist information, luggage lockers and travel agencies. One of DIA's features is unique displays of art and artifacts in such areas as the main terminal, the concourses and the tunnel to the subway. Visitors enjoy big and small artworks including sculptures, large murals, a cactus garden and floor art inlaid with the fossils discovered during the airport's construction. The ecology art in the central space in each of the three concourses is a highlight.

● IMPROVING CONCESSION FACILITIES
Denver International Airport's Concession Program is amied at assuring the highest level of public service and revenue generation, con-sistent with the City and County of Denver's policy of encouraging the participa-tion of Disadvantaged Business Enterprises (DBE). The program encourages quality merchandise, competitive prices and goods and services based upon demonstrated passenger needs. More than one hundred individual concessions, such as restaurants and ordinary plus duty-free shops, are operating in the main terminal and the three concourses—a total area of 13,100 square meters. In the future, the facility may gain a fitnesss center, interactive aviation museums and mountain climbing activity centers. Development of other specialties based on passenger demands is also possible.

Text and Data Contributor
Creg Baker
Public Affairs Officer
Denver International Airport

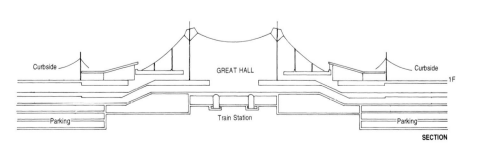

SECTION

世界で最も多忙なメガ空港

シカゴ・オヘア国際空港

アメリカ, イリノイ州, シカゴ

CHICAGO O'HARE INTERNATIONAL AIRPORT
Chicago, Illinois, USA

1. ターミナル1のチケット＆チェックイン・カウンター。スリット天井により自然光を採り入れている
2. 全面ガラス張りの開口部から光が溢れるターミナル5のファサード夜景
3. ターミナル5（国際線用）3階のチケット＆チェックイン・カウンター
1. View of the ticketing & check-in area in the terminal 1
2. Night view of the terminal 5
3. View of the ticketing & check-in area(3F) in the terminal 5

1

C19

EXIT

5

6

4. ヘルムート・ヤーンのデザインによるターミナル1のコンコース
5. シカゴのダウンタウンまで約40分で結ぶCTA地下鉄駅のホーム
6. ターミナル1と3および駐車場を結ぶ通路
7. ターミナル1の2列のコンコースを結ぶ世界一大きなネオン
   彫刻で彩られた地下トンネルと動く歩道
8. 同地下トンネルとインフォメーションボード

4. View of the concourse in the terminal 1
5. Station of CTA train (to downtown) between the
   terminals 2 and 3 on lower level
6. Corridor between the terminals 2 and 3
7. Neon sculpture of the underground tunnel (terminal 1)
8. View of the underground tunnel connecting twin
   concourses of the terminal 1

9. 42のゲートを有するターミナル1のコンコース
9. Concourse of the terminal 1

10. 国際線専用のターミナル5のコンセッションエリア
10. Concession area in the international terminal 5

●世界で最も多忙な空港

シカゴ・オヘア国際空港の歴史は，1940年代初頭，現在の空港がある敷地の一部にあったダグラス航空機会社の生産部門をシカゴ市が買い上げ，新しいランプと誘導路を建設したことに始まる。1949年に市当局は，それまで「オーチャード・プレイス」と呼ばれていた一帯の名前を，第二次世界大戦のシカゴ出身のヒーローである海軍少佐 Edward H. "Butch" O' Hare の名にちなんで新しい空港名とした。現在でもバッゲージ・タッグに記されている省略文字 "ORD"（オーチャード）は，当時の名残りである。オヘア国際空港が国内線商業輸送用空港として正式にオープンしたのは1955年10月のことである。翌年末までに17の定期便が飛ぶようになり，最初の1年間で約16万便，72万人の旅客を扱った。以後，大規模な空港開発計画を経て，1994年には，離発着便数88万3062便，利用総旅客数は世界最大の6646万8269人に上り，「世界で最も多忙な空港」としてその名を馳せている。

●ガラスとスチールによる "明日のターミナル"

1970年代に始まった，アメリカ最大の空港拡張計画の一つ「オヘア開発計画」は，当時大幅に増大してきた空港需要と将来の要求に応えるため，ターミナル，ゲート及びアクセス・システムの新設・拡張を中心に進められた。1984年9月には，空港からシカゴ市のダウンタウンまでを約40分で結ぶCTA地下鉄が開通し，低料金，直接乗り入れのアクセスが実現した。開通以来10年間で，2100万人を超える乗客がこの電車を利用している。1987年8月には，シカゴの著名な建築家ヘルムート・ヤーンの設計により "明日のターミナル"（ターミナル1）が完成した。平行に配列された全長1600フィート（約488m）の2本のコンコースは，ガラスとスチールによるハイテックな美しさと陽光にあふれた空間を生み出し，旅客を

楽しませている。2列のコンコースは，有名な世界一大きなネオン彫刻で彩られた地下トンネルで結ばれている。また，1990年5月には，古い設備を一掃し，ターミナル3が完全リニューアル・オープン。さらに1993年5月には国際線専用の新しいターミナル5がオープンした。同時期に各ターミナル間を結ぶシャトル・トレイン（ATS＝Airport Transit System）も完成し，シカゴ・オヘア国際空港は，四つのターミナルビル（ターミナル1・2・3・5）で全162ゲートを有する，「世界で最も多忙な空港」に相応しい偉容と，安全性，サービスと効率性において世界的な水準を保つ空港となった。

●三つのテーマで開発された国際線コンセッション

商業・サービス施設は，主として三つの国内線ターミナルにある8本のコンコースと中央の円形広場に，飲食部門は1万1800m²，リテールショップ部門2239m²のコンセッション・エリアを展開している。国際線用のターミナル5にはコンセッション用スペース合計2250m²が確保され，現在商業施設として1560m²が使用されている。国際線ターミナルにおけるコンセッション計画は，外国人旅客をターゲットとして，シカゴ・テーマ（Chicago Theme），ブランディング（Branding），ストリート・プライシング（Street Pricing）という三つの項目に重点が置かれている。シカゴ・テーマは，シカゴの地域性をアピールする商品構成を行うなどして，シカゴを出発する旅客に対し，シカゴの良さを印象づけることが目標とされている。例えば，レストラン・エリアに設置されたビデオ・ウォールからは，シカゴ市の文化施設，建築の提示，新しい伝統や人々の絶え間ないプレゼンテーションが流されている。ブランディングは，旅客の母国語が必ずしも英語でないことを考慮して，商品の価格や品質が瞬時に分かるよう提供すること。そしてストリート・プライシングは，空港内での購買価格に

客観性を持たせ，安心して買い物ができるように，ターミナルでの価格を地域社会での価格とほとんど同額に保つようにすることである。コンセッション・プランは，中央集合化プランを採用しており，ターミナルの中心に位置した限られた数の店舗で納得のゆく品質と製品を旅客に提供することに焦点を合わせて，旅客の利便性と購買意欲の両方を満足させている。

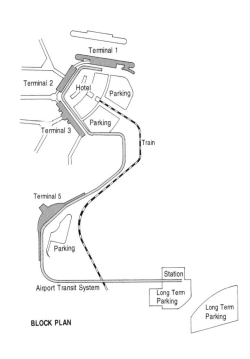

BLOCK PLAN

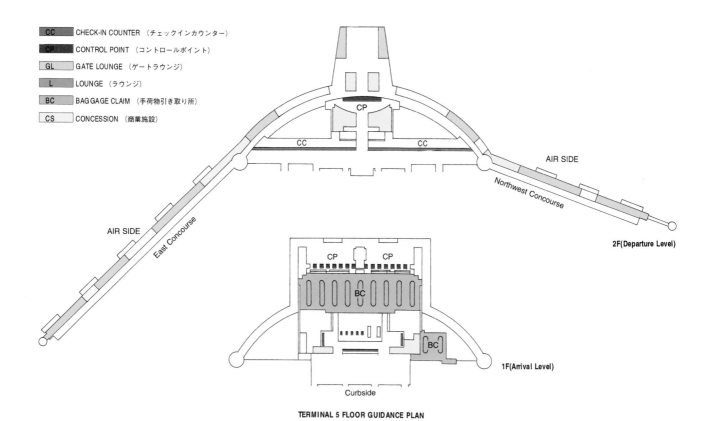

CC   CHECK-IN COUNTER　（チェックインカウンター）
CP   CONTROL POINT　（コントロールポイント）
GL   GATE LOUNGE　（ゲートラウンジ）
L   LOUNGE　（ラウンジ）
BC   BAGGAGE CLAIM　（手荷物引き取り所）
CS   CONCESSION　（商業施設）

TERMINAL 5 FLOOR GUIDANCE PLAN

● THE WORLD'S BUSIEST AIRPORT

In the early 1940s, a portion of the site on which O'Hare International Airport now sits was home to the Douglas Aircraft Corporation manufacturing facility. The City of Chicago acquired the site and built new ramps and taxiways. In 1949, the City renamed the airport, which had been known as Orchard Place, after a World War II naval hero from Chicago, Lt. Commander Edward H."Butch" O'Hare. A reminder of the airport's original name remains in the "ORD" abbreviation, which is used today on all airline baggage tags.

O'Hare was officially opened to domestic commercial traffic in October 1955. By the end of 1956, 17 scheduled airlines were operating out of the airport. During its first full year of operation, O'Hare handled approximately 160,000 flights and 723,296 passengers. In 1994, O'Hare handled 883,062 flights and 66,468,269 passengers, the highest volume of any airport in the world. Consequently, O'Hare is commonly known as "The World's Busiest Airport." The airport is determined to further its tradition of being among the world's very best by adhering to its goals of safety and security; customer service and user friendliness; environmental responsibility; cleanliness; and efficiency of operation and cost.

● "TERMINAL FOR TOMORROW" DESIGNED WITH GLASS AND STEEL

In the 1970s, to meet increasing demand, one of the nation's largest airport expansion programs, the O'Hare Development Program was designed to upgrade the airport's terminals, gates and access systems. In September 1984, an inexpensive, direct train link between the airport and Chicago's downtown area was inaugurated. The trip takes 40 minutes and more than 21 million people boarded trains at O'Hare in the ten years since its opening.

By August 1987, the O'Hare Development Program was 75% complete, as United Airlines "Terminal for Tomorrow," designed by Chicago's noted architect Helmut Jahn, began full-scale operation. Two 488 meter long parallel concourses, made of glass and steel, create an exciting and pleasing environment for the traveler. The twin concourses are connected by an underground tunnel that features on its ceilng the world's largest neon sculpture.

In May 1990, some existing structures such as Terminal 3 were given completely new faces through attractive upgrades including new gate design and the addition of skylights. In May 1993, Terminal 5, the airport's new International Terminal, was opened. That same year, O'Hare celebrated the completion of the Airport Transit System (ATS), a light rail system that runs between the terminals. With 162 gates and four terminal buildings (Terminals 1, 2, 3 and 5), O'Hare is not only the world's busiest airport, but also one that sets a global standard for safety, technological advancement, service and efficiency.

●CONCESSIONS AT THE INTERNATIONAL TERMINAL DEVELOPED WITH THREE THEMES

The three domestic terminals, with eight concourses and the Rotunda, contain 11,800 square meters devoted to food and beverage service, and 2,239 square meters devoted to retail operations. In the International Terminal, a total of 2,250 square meters are devoted to food concessions, with 1,560 square meters currently in use for operating commercial establishments. The concession plan for the International Terminal was developed with foreign passengers in mind and is based on three key concepts: Chicago themes, branding and street pricing.

The first was selected to help ensure that passengers leave Chicago with a positive final impression of the city. To accomplish this, merchandise from the local area is emphasized, and a video wall in the food court seating area runs a continuous presentation highlighting the City's cultural institutions, architectural features, traditions and people. An emphasis on brand-name goods affords instant recognition of quality and value, a particularly important attribute in stores where the customers'primary language is not necessarily English. The concept of street pricing was selected to improve purchase value in the airport. Passengers should feel secure that the prices in the terminal are similar to prices in the community.

The Concession Plan focuses on providing passengers with recognizable quality and product variety from a limited number of stores in a centralized concession area. This centralized design is more convenient and actually stimulates purchases.

Text and Data Contributor
Lisa Eilers
Public Rerations Representative
Chicago O'hare International Airport

都市の発展とともに成長する全米有数のリゾート空港

フェニックス・スカイハーバー国際空港

アメリカ，アリゾナ州，フェニックス

PHOENIX SKY HARBOR INTERNATIONAL AIRPORT
Phoenix, Arizona, USA

1. 空港の周回道路東側より見たターミナル4遠景
2. ターミナル4の南側カーブサイド
3. 南側ゲートへ向かうコンコースからターミナル4のメーンビルディングを見る。
   ガラス面にはアートワークの一つとして飛行機の設計図がエッチングされている
1. View of the terminal 4 from the east side
2. South curbside of the terminal 4
3. View of the terminal 4 from the south side concourse

1

4

5

6

4、5. ターミナル4の3階中央にあるフードコート＆コンセッションエリア。
　　中央には等身大のアートワークが配されている
6. ターミナル3の西側メザニンレベルから2階のデパーチャーホールを見る

4、5. Concession area of the terminal 4
6. View of the departure hall in the terminal 3

TOUCHDOWN at Sky Harbor

7

8

9

7、8．1996年にフェニックスで開催されるスーパーボールをモチーフにしたアートワーク "Touch Down at Sky Harbor" の一つ
9．ターミナル各所に配されたアートワーク
10．ターミナル3の2階コンセッションエリア中央プラザにある噴水を囲んだラウンジ席
7、8．Exhibition entitled "Touch Down at Sky Harbor" in commemoration of Phoenix's first Super Bowl
9．One of the art collections displayed throughout the terminals
10．View of the plaza in the terminal 3 (2F)

11

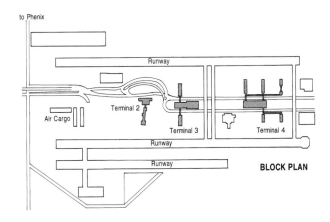

to Phenix

Runway

Terminal 2
Air Cargo
Terminal 3
Terminal 4

Runway

Runway

BLOCK PLAN

●砂漠と山に囲まれた環境
冬の避寒地として全米でも有数のリゾート地であり、南西アメリカの拠点として全米7番目の大都市にまで急速に発展を遂げているアリゾナ州フェニックス。ダウンタウンまで車で約10分という至近距離に位置するフェニックス・スカイハーバー国際空港は、グランドキャニオンやモニュメントバレー、セドナなど豊かな大自然を背景にした多彩なリゾートの玄関口として、また南西アメリカの商業輸送のハブとして、フェニックス市の発展とともに、その姿を大きく変えてきた。フェニックス・スカイハーバー国際空港の歴史は、フェニックス市がまだ山と砂漠に囲まれた荒涼とした小さな町にすぎなかった1935年に、市がAcme投資会社から285エーカーの土地と数棟のビルを購入したことに始まる。当時のスカイハーバー空港は"農場"というニックネームで呼ばれ、パイロットは放牧中の牛を追い払うため、着陸前にいったん低空飛行をしなければならなかったという。

●都市の発展と共にアメリカ有数の空港へと成長
1952年にターミナル1が建設された当時の空港利用客数は約30万人であったが、約10年後にはその数は約3倍となり、ターミナル2が新たに建設された1962年には100万人を超えた。

その後もスカイハーバー空港はフェニックス市の急速な成長と共に、空港施設の拡張・新ターミナル建設を繰り返し、1979年にはターミナル3が建設され、さらに1990年にはターミナル4が完成し、それにともなって老朽化したターミナル1が閉鎖され、現在に至っている。現在、ゲート数は90ゲート、1994年のスカイハーバー空港の総利用者数は2560万人を数え、この数は全米では12番目、世界では18番目の巨大空港に成長した。7層からなる最新のターミナル4は、4本のコンコースと48のゲートを持ち、将来的には8本のコンコース、82のゲートにまで容易に拡張できるようにあらかじめデザインがなされている。ターミナル外壁のレリーフやインテリアには、かつてのサウスウエスタン・プエブロ・スタイル風の文様が反復して使用され、建築デザインの一つの特徴となっている。将来計画としては、急成長し、ますます洗練されていくビジネスやレジャー旅行者に、より高度なサービスの提供が続けられるよう、新たなマスタープランを作成中である。

●アート展示に力を注ぐ
フェニックス・スカイハーバー空港のもう一つの大きな特徴は、ターミナル内の随所に見られるアートワークであろう。招待アーティストによる作品展示か

ら、フェニックスの学生・児童の作品まで、1988年1月以来、120回以上のアート・エキシビションが空港内で行われている。またフェニックス芸術委員会のセレクトによるパーマネント・コレクションの作品のほか、同時に大きなテーマ設定のもとに毎年3回の企画展が催されている。その一つとして、1996年1月、フェニックスが初のNFLスーパーボウルの開催地になったこともあり、"Touch Down at Sky Harbor"と題した大規模な展示会が開催された。これらを含めたスカイハーバーでのアート展示の数は全米随一であるという。

11. ターミナル3の2階デパーチャーホールから南側ゲートへの通路を見る
11. View of the south concourse from departure hall in the terminal 3

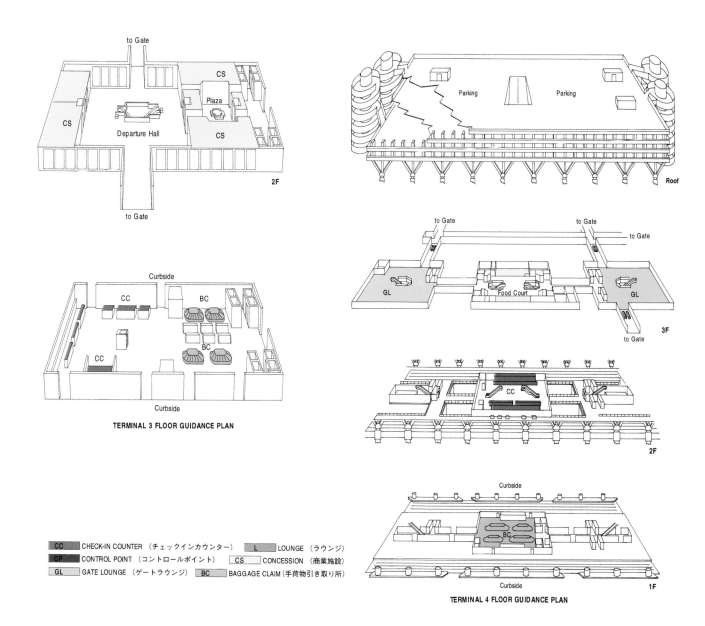

2F

Roof

to Gate

to Gate

CS

Plaza

CS

CS

Departure Hall

CS

Parking

Parking

to Gate

to Gate

to Gate

GL

Food Court

GL

3F

to Gate

Curbside

CC

BC

BC

CC

Curbside

TERMINAL 3 FLOOR GUIDANCE PLAN

CC

2F

Curbside

BC

Curbside

1F

TERMINAL 4 FLOOR GUIDANCE PLAN

CC	CHECK-IN COUNTER （チェックインカウンター）	L	LOUNGE （ラウンジ）
CP	CONTROL POINT （コントロールポイント）	CS	CONCESSION （商業施設）
GL	GATE LOUNGE （ゲートラウンジ）	BC	BAGGAGE CLAIM（手荷物引き取り所）

●A DYNAMIC DESERT PORT

Phoenix, Arizona, one of the foremost winter resort destinations in the United States, has rapidly developed into the seventh biggest city in the nation. Phoenix Sky Harbor International Airport, ten minutes from downtown Phoenix by car, is surrounded by a vast, rich and natural environment that includes one of the seven wonders of the world—the Grand Canyon, also Monument Valley and Sedona. As a resort gateway and the hub of commercial aviation in the southwest region, the airport has largely grown and changed with the city of Phoenix.

●FROM DUSTY RUNWAYS TO STATE-OF-THE-ART AIR SERVICE FACILITY

Sky Harbor got its start when the city purchased 285 acres of land and a few buildings from the Acme Investment Company in 1935. At the time, Phoenix was a small rugged town surrounded by mountains and desert. The airport was first called "The Farm." Pilots had to buzz the field before landing to clear it of grazing cows. This isolated, rural facility emerged as one of the nation's major pasesenger airports in 1952

with the dedication of Terminal 1. The airport was used by nearly 300,000 passengers during that year, and less than ten years, passenger usage tripled. In 1962, when Terminal 2 was opened, the airport broke the 1 million passenger mark. Terminal 2, designed by Paul Coze,won applause as the nation's most beautiful terminal at the time of its completion. The terminal's design expresses not only beauty, but also the airport's dedication to service and flexibility.

As Phoenix business and tourism markets grew, so did Sky Harbor. In 1979, Terminal 3 opened, and Terminal 4 opened its doors to the public in 1990. The seven-tiered, ultra-modern Terminal 4 has 48 gates in four concourses.It is designed to accommodate expansion to 82 gates and eight concourses. With the new terminal in service, Terminal 1 was closed.

In 1994, the airport served more than 25.6 million passengers utilizing 90 gates in total. This figure made Sky Harbor the 12th biggest airport in the United States and the 18th biggest in the world.

Sky Harbor International Airport remains future-oriented. The airport's new master plan will ensure that it continues to provide the highest quality service to an increasingly sophisticated business and leisure traveler.

●SERVING THE ARTS IN STYLE

Sky Harbor also features a substantial art collection displayed throughout the terminals. More than 120 exhibits have been professionally curated since the Sky Harbor Art Program was initiated in 1988. A wide variety of artwork, created by some of the Southwest's most well-known artists, also new artists and children as well, are displayed at the airport. Its permanent collection is augmented by three major exhibitions per year. One of this year's exhibits is entitled "Touchdown at Sky Harbor" Football-related works will be shown in commemoration of Phoenix's first Super Bowl, to be held in January 1996. The exhibitions at Sky Harbor have been appraised as the best of any airport in the United States.

Text and Data Contributor
Joan D.McHenry:Public Information Officer
Phoenix Sky Harbor International Airport

パリ シャルル・ド・ゴール空港

フランス，パリ，ロワシー

CHARLES DE GAULLE AIRPORT
Roissy, Paris, France

1. ターミナル2。ホールC2階の出発ラウンジから開口部越しにエアサイドを見る
   到着と出発の旅客動線を変えるためフィンガーが上下する機構を備えている
2. ターミナル1のサテライト
3. TGVや近郊急行線が乗り入れる鉄道駅の中央ホール吹き抜け
1. View of airside from the hall C(the terminal 2)
2. View of satellite in the terminal 1
3. View of the central hall in the TGV station

1

4

5

4. ターミナル1。チューブエスカレーターに乗り、
   出発階の2階へと向かう
5、7. ターミナル1の上層階に位置するビジネスラ
   ウンジ
6. ターミナル1。この空港の名物ともいえるターミ
   ナルビル中央の円筒形外部空間を縦横に走るチ
   ューブエスカレーター
4. View of tube escalator toward transfer
   level in the terminal 1
5、7. View of the business lounge in the
   terminal 1
6. View of the central area in the terminal 1

8

9

8. 鉄道駅を覆うガラスの大屋根。下に線路とプラットホームがある
9. プラットホームに停車するTGV
10. 鉄道駅の2階レベルからコンコースを見る
11. プラットホームのサインポールと待合椅子

8. View of the big glass roof on the TGV station
9. Platform in the TGV station
10. View of concourse in the TGV station
11. The sign pole on the platform

12

13

12. ターミナルからおよそ車で5分ほどの場所にある
「空港資料館」。空港に関する歴史や環境対策な
どが写真やビデオなどで展示されており，一般
に開放されている
13. ターミナル2のホールCと鉄道駅を結ぶ途中に
あるテレフォンブース
14. 空港駅から一つめのロワシーポール駅周辺では
現在，空港を中心としたビジネスタウン計画が進
行中で，この施設がメーンとなるオフィスコンプ
レックス「ル・ドーム」
12. View of "The Environmental Resource
Center"
13. View of the telephonebooth between the
hall C and TGV station
14. View of the office complex "Le dome"

14

●ターミナル・デザイン三つの世代
シャルル・ド・ゴール空港（以下CDG）は，1日に
およそ1000余りの航空機と10万人余りの旅客，およ
び数千にのぼる車両などを受け入れる巨大空港であ
る。その機能を果たすターミナル施設は現在，CDG-
1ターミナルとその西側に位置するCDG-2（Aから
Dまで）の四つのターミナルホールで，将来その並
びに建設されるターミナル（EとF）を合わせた合
計三つのターミナルがCDGを構成する要素となる。
それぞれのターミナルが各時代を反映しており，ター
ミナル・デザインにおける三つの世代を表してい
る。CDG-1ターミナルがオープンしたのは1974年。
'60年代の高度成長期に設計されたこのパンケーキ形
のターミナルは斬新で，空港デザイン界に新風を巻
き起こした。設計者たちは，迅速な業務と歩行時間
の短縮を考え，さまざまな施設（出発・到着ロビー，
レストラン，店舗，オフィス，駐車場など）を中央
の円筒形の中に積み重ね，それを地下歩道で連結，
七つのサテライトへの直接で迅速なアクセスを提供
した。しかしCDG-1は，そのような強力で複合的な
設計にもかかわらず，円形状のため，それ以上どの
ような拡張も受け付けないという構造上の限界があ
った。そのため，新しいCDG-2のために考えられた
構造が，モジュール方式のターミナルビルであった。

●リング形に連結された四つのターミナルホール
CDG-2では，ターミナル入り口から航空機まで迅速
で簡易なトランジットができることが強調されてい
る。リング形に連結されたCDG-2は，1981年にター
ミナル2Bが，翌年1982年に2Aが，1989年に2D
が，そして1993年に2Cが完成。国際線専用のCDG-
2では，到着旅客と出発旅客の流れが完全に分かれ
ている。また，コンピューターによる手荷物区分け
装置やターミナル各所にデスクを配置したことなど
により，旅客は時間に縛られることなく迅速にチェ
ックインが行えるようになった。1997年オープン予
定の新ターミナル2Fでは，自然採光が重視され，
旅客にとって見通しがよく，分かりやすい空間構成
といった現存のターミナルの粋を集めた革新的なター
ミナルになる予定である。具体的には，ターミナ
ルの長さが現在の200mから400mに拡張され，年間
700万人から1000万人の旅客を扱うことが可能とな
る。また，歩行距離も入り口からパブリックエリア
やチェックインデスクまで45m，チェックインから
出国の場所まで100mという距離になる。

●複合交通基地 "インターモダル・コンプレックス"
CDG-2のAからDまでの四つのホールと，未来の
E・Fの二つのホールの間に完成したのが空港交通の
中心部となるインターモダル・コンプレックスである。
世界でも初めてのこの交通基地は，地下に鉄道駅，
建物上部には楕円形のホテルが造られ，航空機，
電車（TGVおよび郊外電車），そしてターミナル間
を結ぶミニ地下鉄「ピープル・ムーバー」のネット
ワークをすべてここに集結させた多層構造となって
いる。つまり乗客は，気分により，また天候，時
刻，その他の状況により，どの交通機関に頼るかを
自由に選ぶことができるのである。この巨大な施
設は，航空旅行と鉄道旅行のシンボルを調和させ
たもので，4層構造，総床面積10万m²を誇る。空
港駅を覆っている天井は，ハイライトのひとつで
ある2万2000m²のガラス構造で，見上げるとホー
ルC，Dへと連結している歩行者通路を歩く人々
の姿や，その上に建つホテルに向かう人々のダイ
ナミックな動きを目にすることができるのが特徴
である。

15. ターミナル2を俯瞰する。手前が2Bでその左が2D，奥がそれぞれ2Aと2C
15. Bird's-eye view of the terminal 2

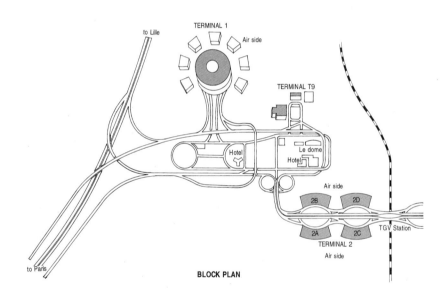

BLOCK PLAN

●THREE GENERATIONS OF TERMINAL
  DESIGN
Charles de Gaulle Airport (CDG) is a huge
complex that can handle more than 1,000
aircraft and 100,000 passengers per day.
CDG's terminal design forms three major units
—the CDG-1 terminal, the CDG-2 (A, B, C
and D terminals), located west of the transport
hub (interconnective exchange unit), and the
two future terminals (E and F) to the east.
These facilities represent three generations of
terminal design, each of which expresses a
design concept particular to its period.

CDG-1, opened in 1974, was designed during
the high-growth years of the 1960s. The
pancake-shaped terminal was a sensational
new departure in airport design. To speed up
operations and reduce walking distance for
passengers, the designers stacked all the
different services—arrivals, departures,
restaurants, shops, offices and parking areas
—on top of one another in a central cylinder.

The terminal is linked by underground
walkways to seven satellite areas, offering
direct, rapid access to the planes. Although
CDG-1 represents a powerful, multifaceted
design concept, it is limited by the circularity of
its structure, which prevents any form of
expansion. For that reason the second
terminal complex is designed on modular
principles.

●FOUR TERMINALS LINKED IN A RING-
  TYPE STRUCTURE
CDG-2's new ring-type structure affords
speedy and easy transit between the terminal
entrance and the planes. The B terminal
opened in 1981, followed by A in 1982, D in
1989 and C in 1993.

Devoted to international and domestic traffic,
the new facility ensures that arriving and
departing passenger flows are completely
separated. With computerized luggage sorting
plus check-in desks scattered throughout the

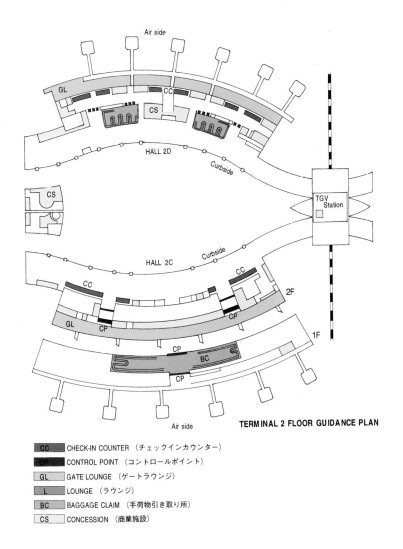

Air side

GL
CC
CS
CS
HALL 2D
Curbside
TGV Station
HALL 2C
Curbside
CC
CC
CP
2F
GL
CP
1F
CP
CP
BC
CP

Air side

TERMINAL 2 FLOOR GUIDANCE PLAN

CC	CHECK-IN COUNTER （チェックインカウンター）
CP	CONTROL POINT （コントロールポイント）
GL	GATE LOUNGE （ゲートラウンジ）
L	LOUNGE （ラウンジ）
BC	BAGGAGE CLAIM （手荷物引き取り所）
CS	CONCESSION （商業施設）

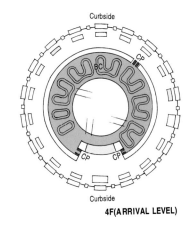

Curbside
BC
CP
CP
CP
Curbside

4F(ARRIVAL LEVEL)

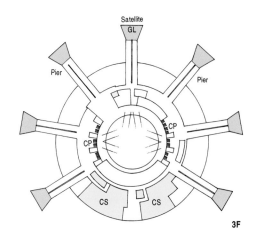

Satellite
GL
Pier
Pier
CP
CP
CS
CS

3F

Curbside

2F(DEPARTURE LEVEL)

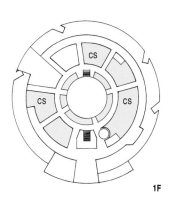

CS
CS
CS

1F

TERMINAL 1 FLOOR GUIDANCE PLAN

terminal, passengers are no longer obliged to check-in at specified times.

CDG-2E and 2F are under construction. 2F, which should be completed in 1997, will bring together the best aspects of the existing terminals, with yet more innovations. The new terminals will be 400 meters long, twice the length of the present terminals, with a capacity of seven to 10 million passengers a year. The two terminals are also designed for ease of passenger movement. The distance between the entrance and check-in desks, for example, is 45 meters; from check-in to embarkation, only 100 meters.

●THE INTERMODAL COMPLEX— A TRANSPORT HUB

Located between the first four units of CDG-2 and the two terminals now being built is a state-of-the-art traffic center for the whole airport— the intermodal complex. This sophisticated transport hub, topped by an

oval-shaped hotel, is the only one of its kind in the world. It brings together planes, trains— the high-speed TGV as well as others—and the mini-metro, a "people mover" network connecting the terminals. Passengers can thus more easily choose a mode of tranportation based on other considerations, such as personal preference, the weather or timetables.

This four-level giant facility, with a total floor area of 100,000 square meters, integrates travel by air and train. The train station is covered by a 22,000-square-meter glass roof, which is one of the highlights of the entire structure. Rail passengers can look up through the roof and see airport users moving on the passageways linking C and D terminals and the hotel.

Data Contributor
Jacques Reder
Press Officer
Aeroports de Paris(ADP)

ヒューマンタッチの温もりを追求した北欧へのゲートウエー

コペンハーゲン空港

デンマーク，コペンハーゲン，カストロップ

COPENHAGEN AIRPORT
Kastrup,Denmark

1. 新設されたGピアのボーディングゲートまわり
2. 空港1階中央部のカーブサイドに面したアライバルホール
1. View of the boarding lounge of new G pier
2. View of the arrival hall

1

2

3

4

5

3. カーブサイドまわり。右がターミナルビル，左がパーキングビル
4. Gピアのボーディングゲート脇のラウンジ席
5. ２階デパーチャーフロアの二つのコンセッションエリアを結ぶ通路
6. ロイヤル・コペンハーゲンやジョージ・ジェンセンなどのデンマークの名品が並ぶコ
　　ンセッションエリア。サインは有名なチボリ公園をモチーフにデザインされている
3. View of the curbside
4. A boarding lounge of new G pier
5. A corridor between two concession areas on the departure floor
6. View of the shopping area on the departure floor

6

7

8

7. ２階デパーチャーフロアに設けられた子供のため
   の遊戯エリア "Kid's Paradise"
8. Ｇピアのボーディングゲート脇ラウンジ席
9. 無数のプラスチックボールで満たされた子供のた
   めの遊戯エリア "Kid's Paradise"
10. セキュリティーコントロールを受けた後に使用す
    る手荷物用カート
11. ラウンジ席各所には格調を感じさせる北欧モダ
    ン家具が配されている
7. 9. "Kid's Paradise" on the departure floor
8. View of the boarding lounge in new G pier
10. Carts for the small baggage
11. Scandinavian modern furniture for the
    boarding lounge

9

10

11

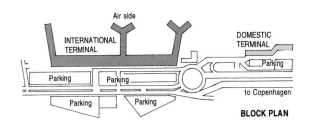

Air side

INTERNATIONAL
TERMINAL

DOMESTIC
TERMINAL

Parking

Parking | Parking

Parking

Parking | Parking

to Copenhagen

BLOCK PLAN

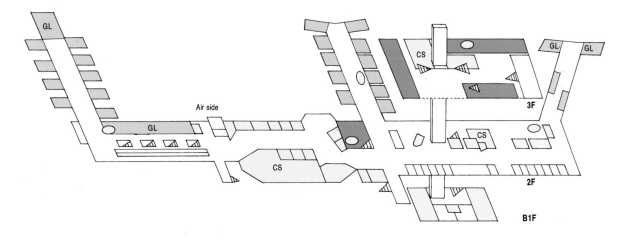

GL

GL

Air side

GL

CS

CS

CS

GL | GL

CS

3F

2F

B1F

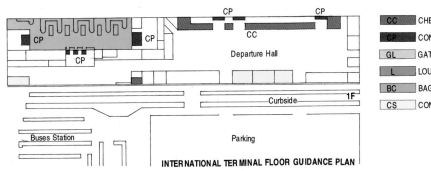

CP | CP | CP

CP

CC

CP

CP

Departure Hall

Curbside | 1F

Buses Station

Parking

INTERNATIONAL TERMINAL FLOOR GUIDANCE PLAN

CC	CHECK-IN COUNTER	（チェックインカウンター）
CP	CONTROL POINT	（コントロールポイント）
GL	GATE LOUNGE	（ゲートラウンジ）
L	LOUNGE	（ラウンジ）
BC	BAGGAGE CLAIM	（手荷物引き取り所）
CS	CONCESSION	（商業施設）

●世界初の民間空港

コペンハーゲン市街から南東へ約8km、バルト海に面し、市街地と橋で結ばれたアマガー島にこの空港は位置している。カストロップ空港と呼ばれていたこのエアポートが、1924年に世界で初めての民間人のためだけの空港としてオープンした時は、粗末な木造の建物と水上飛行機用の小波止場、それに2～3棟の小格納庫、草の上に滑走路が2本あっただけであった。第2次世界大戦後は戦争中に被害を受けなかった数少ない飛行場の一つとして発展を続け、やがてジェット機時代を迎えることとなった。現在の空港施設は、1980年代、90年代の拡張計画によりトランスファー区域は2倍以上になり、ヨーロッパでもっとも美しいトランスファー・ショッピングセンターが増築された。また、国内線ターミナルも2倍に拡張され、ランドサイドの諸設備は新アクセス道路および駐車場ビルの建設により改善された。将来の計画としては、トラフィックセンターの建設が予定され、また現存のターミナル施設、周辺施設、新鉄道駅などを含む総合建設計画により2000年までには鉄道やハイウエーとリンクされる予定である。

●旅客ではなくゲストが訪れる空港

北欧といえば、人々は森と湖に囲まれた美しい自然を持つ国家、福祉の行き届いた住み心地の良さ、清潔で治安の良い都市、シンプルだが質の高いスカンジナビアン・デザインなどをイメージする。コペンハーゲン空港は、それらに代表される北欧のイメージを見事に体現し、デンマークを訪れる旅人を温かく迎え入れ、ホッとした気分にさせてくれる。空港はデンマーク政府を主要株主とする法人によって運営されているが、その理念は、この空港を訪れるのは1500万人の旅客ではなく、1500万人のゲストであるということが基本になっている。それぞれに異なった個人としての要求を持ったゲストに対してホストとして最上のものを提供するという考えのもとに"空港らしくない空港""あなたが満足するように""何のトラブルも起きない"というコンセプトが、施設のデザインから運営の小さな事柄の隅々に至るまで追求されている。旅客の安全の確保についても、「旅客一人の問題は全員の問題」というモットーの下に、空港スタッフは取り組んでいる。

●自然光をふんだんに取り入れた建築空間

コペンハーゲン空港の建築は、緑の植物やモダンアートに囲まれたリラックスできる環境を創出するために、自然採光を大胆に取り入れている。旅行者は常にストレスを感じながら移動しているのであり、それを取り除くためには快適さとリラクセーションが必須条件なのである。事実、空港のロビーやモー

ルは最新のショッピングセンターと一流のホテルを合体させたような雰囲気であり、さりげなくそこここに配された椅子などの家具は高名な北欧のデザイナーの手になる逸品揃いである。コンセッションとしては、小さな壜類から自動車のボルボまでを扱う30以上の店舗を持つショッピングセンター、軽食から豪華なディナーまでのグレードにわかれた18店のレストラン、バー。仮眠室、日光浴用のデッキチェア、サウナまでもあるトランジットホテルなどを持ち、"来客が快適性を求めて喜んでお金を使うことは健全な投資である"というポリシーのもと、細かく行き届いたサービスを提供している。

12. エアサイドから見たボーディングゲート
13. 新設のGピアをエアサイドから見る
12. External view from the airside
13. View of new G pier from the airside

12

13

● WORLD'S FIRST CIVIL AIRPORT

Copenhagen Airport, 8 kilometers from downtown, is located on Amager Island, connected to the town by bridges. It faces the Baltic Sea. The airport was opened in 1925 as the world's first civil airport and named Kastrup Airport. It was then nothing more than a wooden barracks, a quay for waterborne aircraft, a few small hangars and a couple of runways but later in 1939 a modern airport was build.

The airport was one of the few undamaged during World War II, and its continuing growth soon carried it into the jet age. New terminal was built in 1960, and In expansion projects during the 1980s and 1990s, the transfer area was doubled, and Europe's most beautiful transfer shopping center was created. The area of the domestic terminal was also doubled, and the landside facilities were improved with new access roads and a multi-storied parking area.

Future expansion will include construction of a intermodal traffic centre and extension of the international terminal facilities by the year 2000. Copenhagen Airport will be linked to the Scandinavian peninsula and Germany by rail and highway.

● AIRPORT VISITED BY GUESTS, NOT PASSENGERS

When people think of Scandinavia, they often envision beautiful countryside with forests and lakes, or clean, peaceful, orderly cities, or the countries' noted social systems, or even the simple, understated elegance of Scandinavian design. Copenhagen Airport expresses many of those images in its design. It warmly welcomes travelers.

The airport is run by a private company, with the Danish government as the major shareholder. The company's management philosophy is expressed in its motto: "We don't have 15 million passengers every year, we are visited by 15 million guests evey year." Copenhagen Airport offers its guests the very best. The management company has instilled three concepts in service: "the non-airport airport," "do as you please" and "no problem." These concepts are apparent in the small details of the airport's operation, and even in the airport's design. The airport's security operations are also based on a saying: "A guest's problem is every staff person's problem."

● ARCHITECTURAL SPACE FILLED WITH NATURAL LIGHT

Copenhagen Airport's modern architecture and design create a friendly atmosphere. Well-arranged greenery, modern art and plenty of natural light add charm and relieve stressed-out travelers. The facilities resemble a cross between a modern shopping center and a luxury hotel. The casually arranged designer furniture contributes to the relaxed atmosphere.

The shopping center has 30 stores, offering everything from notions to Volvo's, as well as 18 restaurants and bars. Other services include a transit hotel equipped with slumber cabins, sun beds and saunas. Management believes that investing in a higher level of comfort is sound, because travelers will appreciate the difference and consequently the rate of transfer passengers (today 42%) will increase even more.

Text and Data Contributor
Bo Haugaard
Director,Marketing,PR and Cargo
Copenhagen Airport

伝統的なデザインを取り入れたガーデン・エアポート

ジャカルタ・スカルノ・ハッタ国際空港

インドネシア，ジャカルタ

JAKARTA SOEKARNO-HATTA INTERNATIONAL AIRPORT
Jakarta, Indonesia

1. 国際線用第2ターミナルのカーブサイド夕景
2. 第1ターミナルを管制塔より遠望する
3. 第2ターミナルのカーブサイドとパーキングエリア
1. Evening view of the curbside in front of the international terminal 2
2. View of the terminal 1 from the control tower
3. View of the curbside in front of the international terminal 2

1

2

3

4

5

4. ターミナル2のボーディングラウンジに続くコリドーの吹き抜けに配された照明器具
5. ショッピング施設が並ぶターミナル2のトランジットラウンジ
6. ボーディングラウンジのインテリア
7. 通路側からボーディングラウンジを見る。周囲には「ガーデンエアポート」のコンセプトにふさわしく亜熱帯の植物が生い茂る「庭園」が配されている
4. View of the corridor towards the boarding gate
5. Shopping area and transit lounge in the terminal 2
6. Interior of the boarding lounge of the terminal 2
7. View of the boarding lounge from the corridor

●発展するインドネシアの新しい表玄関
ジャカルタ・スカルノ・ハッタ国際空港は、インドネシアの首都ジャカルタの北西に隣接するタンジェラン・リージェンシー（Tangerang Regency）にあり、オープン以来、インドネシアの表玄関として重要な役目を果たしている。1980年初頭までジャカルタでは、国内線専用のクマヨラン空港と、国際線専用のハリム空港の2空港が運用されていたが、インドネシア政府はジャカルタの将来的な航空需要を考慮し、1977年から1979年の間に策定されたマスタープランに基づいて、国際線、国内線の両方を擁する新空港の建設を決定した。新空港は、2400m隔てて独立運用が可能な2本の平行滑走路と、将来的には四つの旅客ターミナルビルが建設可能なように確保された1800haの広大な敷地に、インドネシアとフランス両政府の合同事業として1980年12月に建設がスタートし、4年半の歳月を経て、1985年5月に正式開港となった。新空港がオープンしたことにより、それまでのクマヨラン空港は閉鎖され、ハリム空港は国賓やhaji（巡礼）便などの特別使用として現在も運営されている。

●「庭園」内に配置された二つのモジュール式半円形ターミナル
年間900万人の旅客に対応可能な半円形をした第1ターミナルビルは、エプロンまで3本のピアが伸びており、各ピアに7カ所ずつ、計21の出発ラウンジを持つ。「ガーデン・エアポート」というコンセプトに基づき、ターミナル周辺には熱帯樹木が生い茂り、花々が咲きほこる「庭園」が配され、またフランス人建築家ポール・アンドリューの設計によるターミナルビルは、各所にインドネシアの建築的特徴が十分に生かされている。1985年のオープン以来、ジャカルタの航空需要は増加の一途を辿り、政府ではその伸びに対応すべく、さらに900万人の年間旅客数に対応できる第2ターミナルビルの建設計画が1989年から進められた。第1のターミナルと同様のコンセプト、モジュールによる新ターミナルが1991年10月に完成し、現在の施設構成に至っている。以後、第2ターミナルは国際線およびナショナルフラッグシップキャリアであるガルーダ航空が使用し、第1ターミナルは国内線専用として利用されている。その後も航空需要は増加を続け、1994年の年間旅客数

は第1・2両ターミナル処理能力の75％を占める1250万人に達した。アセアン地区ではシンガポール、クアラルンプール、バンコクの各空港と並んで、国際的なハブ空港として重要な地位を占めている。

●豊かなインドネシア文化を反映したターミナル
二つの旅客ターミナルビルの総床面積は27万6300m²（第1ターミナル：12万5000m²、第2ターミナル：15万1300m²）におよぶが、そのうち8万7300m²が「庭園」で占められ、樹木も成長し「ガーデン・エアポート」としての雰囲気も完成されつつある。これに加えて、搭乗ゲート周辺に設けられた小庭園も、伝統的なデザインが施された外観やインテリアによく合うよう行き届いた管理がなされている。ターミナルのデザインには、インドネシアの多種多様な群島文化が反映されている。例えば、ターミナルのメーン通路の屋根には、カリマンタンの典型的な長い家屋建築が引用され、またインドネシア各地から集められたレリーフや、彫刻、壁画などのさまざまなオーナメントが、ターミナルの各所に反復して配置されてインドネシア文化の豊かさを伝えている。当初、ターミナル内は、ショップやサービス施設のためのスペースが狭いレイアウトとなっていたが、旅客の要求と利便性を満たす、広くて高品質な商品やサービスを提供するコンセッションエリアの新設により、こうした問題も改善されてきている。

8. 壁面にインドネシアの伝統的なレリーフが施されたアライバル用通路
9. ターミナル1遠景
10. ターミナル2のカーブサイド
8. An arrival corridor of the terminal 2 on lower level
9. View of the terminal 1 from the control tower
10. View of the curbside in front of the terminal 2

Soekarno-Hatta/Jakarta International Airport, located in Tangerang Regency adjacent to Jakarta, has played an important role as the main gateway to Indonesia. Until the early 1980s, Jakarta was served by two airports—Kemayoran for domestic operation and Halim for international. However, in consideration of future traffic demands, the government decided to construct a new airport to accommodate international and domestic flights, and thus prepared a master plan between 1977 and 1979.

Construction started in December 1980 as a joint project between Indonesia and France. The new airport was inaugurated in July 1985 as the Soekarno/Hatta Jakarta International Airport. With a total area of 1,800 hectares, the airport's alloted space is large enough to permit construction of four more terminals.

The new facility includes two independently operational runways built 2,400 meters apart. When the new airport was opened, Kemayoran Airport was closed, but Halim Airport still handles domestic flights, including travel by state guests and Muslim pilgrims.

● "GARDEN AIRPORT" —HALF-MOON-SHAPED MODULAR TERMINALS
The half-moon-shaped first terminal, with a capacity of nine million passengers per year, has three piers extended to the apron. Each pier has 7 boarding lounges. Around the terminal, designed based on "Garden Airport" concept, is studded with tropical gardens. And the terminal building, designed by Paul Andrew, a French architect, expresses Indonesian architectural styles.

Because demand grew following the airport's opening in 1985, the Indonesian government decided to construct Terminal 2 to handle an additional nine million passengers per year. Construction started in 1989, and the terminal, employing the same concept and modular system as the first terminal, was completed in

8

October 1991.

Since then Terminal 2 has been used for international flights, including those of Garuda Indonesia, the nation's flagship carrier, while Terminal 1 has been used for domestic flights. Demand has increased steadily, reaching 12.5 million passengers in 1994—72% of the terminals' combined capacity. Thus Jakarta International Airport has played a significant role as an international hub in the ASEAN region, along with Singapore, Kuala Lumpur and Bangkok Airports.

● REFLECTING INDONESIA'S
CHARACTERISTIC CULTURE

Out of the total floor area of 276,308 square meters—125,000 square meters for Terminal 1 and 151,308 square meters for Terminal 2—87,300 square meters are devoted to gardens. As the gardens mature, the "Garden Airport" concept is becoming a reality. In addition, small gardens around the gates are maintained to match the traditional exterior and interior designs of the buildings.

The airport terminals reflect the unity in diversity that is a key attribute of the Indonesian archipelago. The typical long house architecture of Kalimantan, for example, was used for the main corridor's roof structure. Different ornaments from various parts of Indonesia—reliefs, sculptures, murals and statues—enrich the interior and exterior of the terminal buildings, revealing the nation's cultural wealth.

The original floor layout in the terminals provided insufficient space for commercial activities. But the airport recently solved this problem by allocating more space to highly qualified concessionaires, a move intended to meet passengers' wants and needs.

Text and Data Contributor
IR.A.Hendarmin
Director of Airport Engineering,
Directorate General of Air Communications,
Ministry of Communications, Republic Indonesia
Jakarta Soekarno-Hatta International Airpot

9

10

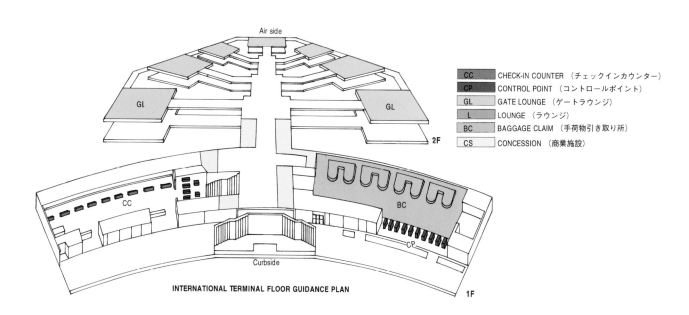

	CHECK-IN COUNTER （チェックインカウンター）
CC	
CP	CONTROL POINT （コントロールポイント）
GL	GATE LOUNGE （ゲートラウンジ）
L	LOUNGE （ラウンジ）
BC	BAGGAGE CLAIM （手荷物引き取り所）
CS	CONCESSION （商業施設）

INTERNATIONAL TERMINAL FLOOR GUIDANCE PLAN

生態環境の保護と技術的発展との相互作用の実現を目指す

チューリッヒ空港

スイス，チューリッヒ

ZURICH AIRPORT
Zurich, Swiss

1

1. エアサイドよりスイス航空の旅客機越しに管制塔を見る
2. ターミナルAのチェックインカウンター・エリア
1. View of the control tower from airside
2. View of the check-in counter in the terminal A

2

3

4

3. ターミナルA・2階出発フロアのショッピングアーケード。正面右手にパスポートコントロールがある
4. 空港内にはアートオブジェがサインとして各所に設置されている
5. ターミナルA・2階の出発ラウンジ。吹き抜けになった上階にはビジネスラウンジがある
6. ターミナルAのゲートへ向かうピアもいくつかのオブジェで彩られている
3. View of the shopping arcade in the terminal A
4. The sign objects
5. View of the departure lounge in the terminal A
6. View of an object in the pier

5

6

7

8

7. ターミナルBの壁面に描かれたジャンボジェットの絵
8. エアポートプラザの地下鉄空港駅。チューリッヒ市内へは約10分
9. ターミナルA・2階の出発ロビーに設置された手提げ袋のサインオブジェ
10. エアポートプラザの吹き抜けになった中央広場

7. Painted wall of the teminal B
8. View of the airport railway station under the Airport Plaza
9. The sign objects in the terminal A
10. View of the central area in the Airport Plaza

●ヨーロッパの上位10空港の一つ
1946年夏に始まったチューリッヒ空港の建設は、ターミナル設備の完成により、1953年8月29日正式にオープンした。チューリッヒ市内から急行でおよそ10分の近郊に位置するこの空港は、80カ国、150以上の都市と結ばれており、1995年の利用客数は1500万人を超え、ヨーロッパの上位10空港の一つに数えられている。集客範囲はスイス国土の半分以上を占め、国境を越えて広がっている。チューリッヒ空港はヨーロッパの中心に位置しているうえ各地と接続しているため、ヨーロッパではポピュラーな国際空港の一つである。チューリッヒ空港駅はスイスの鉄道網と接続しており、都市間列車、特急電車、ローカル線が1日170便以上乗り入れていてスイス全土と結ばれている。この空港からは世界中のどの場所にも24時間以内に着くことができる。
銀行員、サプライヤー、カスタマー、および保険会社、貿易会社などが空港の定期利用客であり、また製造業が国外に移転する動きが活発化しているのにともない、開発エンジニア、サービスマン、営業マ

ンといったスイスのビジネスマンの空港利用も増加している。また、空港駅には商業集積が配置され、ターミナルビル内のコンセッションと合わせて旅客サービスの向上が図られている。

●環境バランスの調査・保全を実施した最初の空港
今日、空港にとって環境保護に積極的にかかわっていくことは重要な課題となっている。チューリッヒ空港では運営によって生じる環境負担（交通量を増やす場合など）を限界内に抑えるための適切な対策を採るようにしている。すでに環境問題については、1990年代初期に環境バランスについての立案をした最初の空港の一つであった。同時にスイス航空も、環境に対する業務の影響を生態バランスに基づいて分析した最初の航空会社であった。この分析をもとに環境保護のためにそれらを実行に移し、生態環境と技術的発展との相互作用の国際的な見本となることを目指している。
また、チューリッヒ空港はこの地域で多くの雇用機会を創出しており、空港のフルタイム従業員は1万

6000人以上、パートタイム従業員は約7000人である。空港は20年以上も利益を出しており、運営に関して納税者に負担をかけない施設となっている。

●「エアポート2000」計画
チューリッヒ空港は、ここ数年の交通量の増加にインフラストラクチャーがついていけなくなり、運営が困難になっていることに対し、1997年から総開発費21億スイスフラン（約1922億円）をかけて「エアポート2000」と名付けられた以下の計画を予定している。
1. 誘導路での追越しレーンの新設
2. 現在の設備にリンクする新しいミッドフィールド・コンコース
   （動く歩道の設置、コンコースの延長など）
3. 乗客ターミナルまでの鉄道駅の開発
   （新しいタイプのショッピングコンコース、バスステーションとの接続など）
4. カーゴ設備及び空港保守基地の開発、新しい多層式駐車場C、改良した道路アクセス
これら最新設備のオープンは2002年が予定されている。

11

12

11. ピア屋上よりエアサイド越しにターミナルビルを見る
12. ターミナルA・出発フロアのカーブサイドを見る
11. View of the terminal building from a roof of the pier
12. View of a curbside in front of the terminal A

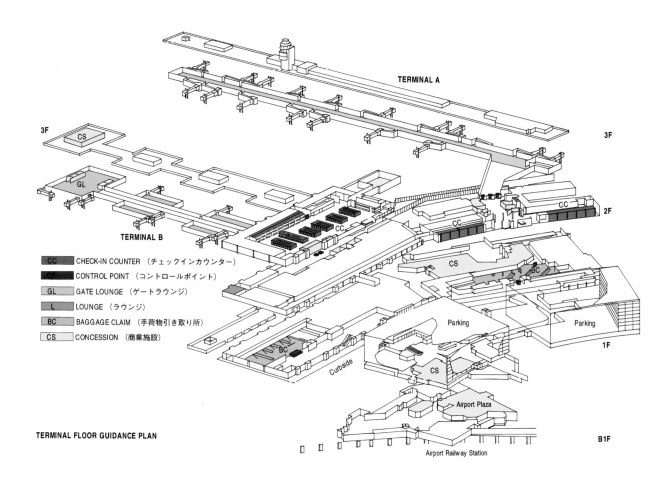

TERMINAL A

3F   3F

GL

TERMINAL B

CC	CHECK-IN COUNTER（チェックインカウンター）
CP	CONTROL POINT（コントロールポイント）
GL	GATE LOUNGE（ゲートラウンジ）
L	LOUNGE（ラウンジ）
BC	BAGGAGE CLAIM（手荷物引き取り所）
CS	CONCESSION（商業施設）

CC   2F

CS   BC

Parking   Parking

1F

BC

Curbside

CS

Airport Plaza

TERMINAL FLOOR GUIDANCE PLAN

B1F

Airport Railway Station

●ONE OF EUROPE'S TEN LARGEST AIRPORTS

Construction began on Zurich Airport in summer 1946. The airport was inaugurated on August 29, 1953.

Located in Kloten, about 10 minutes by train from downtown Zurich, the airport offers flights to more than 160 cities in 80 countries. During 1995 it served more than 15 million passengers, thus becoming one of Europe's ten biggest airports. Its regional market covers an area more than half the size of Switzerland and extends far beyond the country's borders. Its location in central Europe contributes to Zurich Airport's standing as one of the most popular airports in Europe. The airport also boasts a link to the Swiss railway network. Every day more than 170 intercity, express and local trains connect the airport to centers throughout Switzerland.

Travelers leaving the airport via surface transportation can reach most European destinations within 24 hours. All kinds of business people, such as employees of banks, insurance companies and trading

firms, are regular users of the airport. As manufacturing firms increase their international operations, more of their engineers, service and sales people have started using the airport. The commercial area at the airport train station vies with concessions in the terminal, and thus improves selection available to passengers.

●THE FIRST AIRPORT TO ACHIEVE ENVIRONMENTAL PROTECTION

Today, environmental protection is a key aspect of any airport's operations. Zurich Airport has responded accordingly. The airport did pioneering work on environmental problems in the beginning of the 1990s, and the country's national airline, Swissair, was the first to analyze the effect of airline operation on the environment. Zurich Airport aims to be an international example of the balance between ecology and technical achievement.

The airport is the most important employer in the region, with more than 16,000 full time and approximately 7,000 part time employees. The airport has been profitable for more than 20

years and is thus self-supporting.

●AIRPORT 2000 PROJECT

Because of the rapid increase of users over the past several years, the present infrastructure needs expansion. The airport will undergo this expansion starting in 1997 when "Airport 2000" is launched. This expansion program is expected to cost 2.1 billion Swiss francs. The project includes:

1. Overtaking lanes on taxiways
2. A new midfield concourse—to be linked to the present facilities by people mover rail link.
3. Development of the airport railway station into a passenger terminal
4. Development of the cargo facilities and the airport maintenance base, a new multi-storied parking area.

The first of the new facilities will be opened in the year 2002.

Text and Data Contributor
Andreas Meier
Public Relations Department
Zurich Airport Authority

一つ屋根の下にあらゆる都市機能を備えた"エアポート・シティ"

フランクフルト空港

ドイツ，フランクフルト

FRANKFURT AIRPORT

Frankfurt am Main, Germany

1. ターミナル2のシャトルトレイン駅より飲食施設エリア"フードプラザ"を見る
2. フードプラザよりシャトルトレイン駅方向を見る
1. View of Food Plaza from shuttle train Skyline station in the terminal 2
2. View of the shuttle train station from Food Plaza

2

3

4

3. ターミナル2にあるフードプラザのエアサイドに面した客席
4. フードプラザ内の飲食施設カウンターまわり造作
5、6. フードプラザ中央に設けられた子供のための遊戯エリア
3. A dining area of Food Plaza in the terminal 2
4. Order counters of the fast food restaurant in Food Plaza
5、6. View of the children's play area in Food Plaza

5

6

7

8

7. ターミナル2のボーディングラウンジ内コンセッションエリ
   ア。ショップの屋根部分は飛行機の翼がデザインモチーフに
   なっている
8. ターミナル1のチケット＆チェックインエリアのメザニンレ
   ベルにあるエキシビションホール
9. ターミナル1のチケット＆チェックインエリア
10. ターミナル1のデパーチャーフロアにある教会
7. A boarding lounge and concession area of the
   terminal 2
8. An exhibition space on upper level of the terminal 1
9. View of the check-in counter of the terminal 1
10. View of the church on uppper level of the terminal 1

9

10

●旅客数急増に対応する近代化拡張プロジェクト
フランクフルト空港の利用総旅客数は1994年に3510万人を記録した（ヨーロッパではロンドン・ヒースロー空港に次いで2番目、世界では6番目にあたる）。これはターミナル1が最初にオープンした1972年の利用客数1160万人の3倍以上であり、さらに2年後には400万人強の増加が見込まれている。現在、予想される2000年以降の航空輸送量増加に対応するため、大規模な開発が進行している。このプログラムは新しいターミナル2の建設を中心に進められてきたが、それが1994年10月にオープンし、現在は既存のターミナル1の近代化拡張プロジェクトが進行している。フランクフルト空港の利用旅客数が急激に増加したのは、こうしたターミナル設備や様々な乗

客サービスの充実が、効率的に計画、実行されていることがその理由の一つにあげられよう。

●すべてのサービスを一つ屋根の下で
フランクフルト空港の経営戦略であり、ヨーロッパ大陸で最も利用量の多い空港輸送ゲートウエーとして成功している背景にある基本的理念は、「すべてのサービスを一つ屋根の下で」得られるようにすることにある。ターミナル1と2、フランクフルト空港センター（FAC）、シェラトンホテルとコングレスセンターという各施設は、屋外に全く出る必要のない容易なアクセスを利用者に提供しており、新設されたスカイラインと呼ばれるターミナルシャトルを利用すれば、両ターミナル間をわずか数分で移動することが可能である。また同時にターミナル2にまで拡張された自動荷物コンベアシステムにより、フランクフルト空港は二つのターミナルを有するようになったにもかかわらず、人もバッゲージも45分という乗り継ぎ時間が保証されている。
また、航空機と鉄道を複合したトラベル・サービスにおいては、フランクフルト空港はパイオニア的存在である。第1ターミナル地階にある鉄道駅からは、Sバーン（快速列車）によりフランクフルト中央駅まで約12分でアクセスでき、またドイツ国鉄のインターシティ列車で、ドイツ主要都市と結ばれている。さらに今世紀末までには空港第2駅が完成し、ICE（ドイツの高速新幹線）の運行が始まる予定である。

●さらに充実するコンセッション＆サービス施設
フランクフルト空港には、二つのターミナル内だけ

でも150店舗以上の多様なリテールショップ、約40店舗のレストラン、バー、ビストロがテナントとして入っている。その他、ターミナル1地下のドイツ国鉄・空港駅周辺のショッピングセンターやアーケード、ホテルやコングレスセンター内の料飲施設も含めると、日用品から高級ブランド商品まで、ゲストの多様なニーズに十分応え得る商環境を実現している。こうしたショップやレストラン、バーなどの飲食施設以外に、銀行や郵便局はもちろん、医療・ヘルスケア施設、ディスコ、教会、多様な宗教信仰者のための祈とう・黙想室、アミューズメント施設などの様々なサービス施設を併設し、空港自体が一つの都市としての機能を完備した"エアポートシティ"といっても過言ではない。
また、空港内のショッピング施設については、その設計基準として、ショッピングエリアがターミナル内の乗客の大きな流れを妨げないことが第1に考えられている。また、最近の各種コンセッションの選定にあたっては、乗客の購買動態の調査と空港で得た経験に基づき、ターミナルのショッピングモールには、有名ブランド店や明確な方針を持つスペシャリティ・ショップを出店させる傾向にある。その結果、フランクフルト空港内の140以上の営業権取得会社（一部は複数の店舗）からの収入は、1994年に約1億8000万DM（約126億円）にのぼり、特に免税店からの収入は13.3%と二桁増加を果たしている。このような高収入を支えているのは、当空港がターミナル内での来客の迅速で効果的な通行、美的で快適な空間、大混雑のないことなどが確保されていることによるものと考えられている。

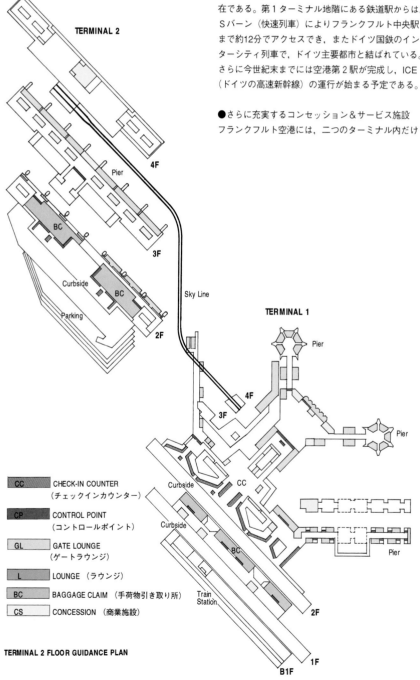

TERMINAL 2

Pier
4F

Pier
3F
BC

Curbside
BC
2F
Parking

Sky Line

TERMINAL 1

Pier
4F
3F
Pier

Curbside
CC

Curbside
BC
Pier

Train
Station
2F

1F

B1F

CC	CHECK-IN COUNTER （チェックインカウンター）
CP	CONTROL POINT （コントロールポイント）
GL	GATE LOUNGE （ゲートラウンジ）
L	LOUNGE （ラウンジ）
BC	BAGGAGE CLAIM （手荷物引き取り所）
CS	CONCESSION （商業施設）

TERMINAL 2 FLOOR GUIDANCE PLAN

11. ターミナル2の送迎デッキ"ビジターズテラス"
12. ターミナル2をエアサイドから見る
11. Airside view from the Visitors terrace
12. External view of the terminal 2 from airside

●MODERNIZATION AND EXPANSION PROJECT IN LINE WITH RAPID PASSENGER GROWTH

In 1994, Frankfurt Airport welcomed more than 35.1 million passengers, second in Europe only to London's Heathrow Airport and the sixth biggest figure in the world. This figure is more than three times the 11.6 million recorded in 1972, when Terminal 1 first opened. More than four million additional passengers were received in the last two years alone. This rapid pace of growth is continuing with 38 million passengers expected in 1995.

To accommodate air traffic growth to the year 2000 and beyond, the airport is in the midst of its biggest expansion to date. The first phase, construction of Terminal 2, was completed in October, 1994. Major modernization and expansion of Terminal 1 is now underway. In November 1995 work started on physically joining the terminals by extending "D" area of Terminal 2 to Terminal 1—to create a single mega— terminal. The rapid growth in passenger traffic can be attributed to a wide range of passenger services available in efficiently planned and operated terminal facilities. Also, the wide choice of connections and airlines is attractive for transfer passengers.

●ALL SERVICES UNDER ONE ROOF

The basic policy of Frankfurt Airport's management is "all services under one roof." This policy contributes to the airport's status as Europe's second busiest gateway. The integrated passenger facilities—Terminals 1 and 2, the Frankfurt Airport Center (FAC), and the Sheraton Hotel and Congress Center— offer easy-to-access services that allow passengers to stay inside. Using the new elevated Sky Line people-mover, passengers can transfer from one terminal to the other within a few minutes. Frankfurt Airport's world-famous automated baggage conveyer system has been expanded to Terminal 2. This system guarantees 45-minute transfer time even with two terminals in operation.

Frankfurt Airport is a pioneer in the travel service system that combines an airport and railway. Access to Frankfurt Central Station from the airport station in the basement of Terminal 1 requires only 12 minutes by express train, called S-Bahn. The airport station is also linked to main cities in Germany via the intercity trains of German Rail. By the end of this century, a second airport station will be opened to accommodate the high-speed(300km/h) superexpress train (ICB).

●MORE PROGRESS IN CONCESSION AND SERVICE FACILITIES

Terminals 1 and 2 have more than 150 retail outlets and restaurants, bars and bistros. With more shops and restaurants around the airport station, the hotel and the congress center, the airport meets guests' needs for everything from daily goods to designer brands. The airport's other services, such as banks, post offices,health care facilities, a disco, a chapel, prayer/ meditation rooms for people of various religious faiths and amusement facilities make Frankfurt Airport truly an "airport city."

A design criterion for shopping areas at Frankfurt is that they should not conflict with primary passenger traffic flow through the terminals. As recent changes in the composition of concessions have shown, management is trying to bring more well-known brands and specialty shops into the shopping areas, based on surveys of passenger purchase behavior and experience gained at other comparable airports.As a result, revenue from the more than 140 concessionaires (some having multiple outlets) at Frankfurt Airport reached DM 180 million in 1994. Revenue from duty-free shops was particularly strong, recording a 13.3% increase over the previous year. Such high revenues from concessions are supported by securing quick and efficient passenger traffic throughout the terminals, offering aesthetically pleasing architectural surroundings and eliminating serious congestion that distracts and disturbs visitors.

Text and Data Contributor
Robert A.Payne
Manager of International Press
Frankfurt Airport

11

12

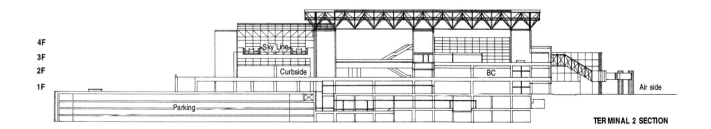

TERMINAL 2 SECTION

観光を意識して独自のローカル・アイデンティティーを表出

バリ・ヌグアライ国際空港

インドネシア，バリ，デンパサール

NGURAH RAI／BALI INTERNATIONAL AIRPORT
Denpasar, Bali, Indonesia

1. 国際線ターミナルビル外観
2. 伝統的なバリの思想を表現した国際線ターミナル中央のフェスティバルプラザ。
　 公務上や観光上の目的で伝統舞踊やセレモニーが披露される場となっている

1. External view of the international terminal from curbside
2. View of the Festival Plaza in the center of the international terminal

1

3. ターミナル中央エアサイドに設けられたバリの寺院建築を引用した割れ門　3. View of the gate, echoing Bali's typical Hindu temple architecture, from airside

4

5

4. フェスティバルプラザの石彫をはじめ通路の腰壁など随所にバリの伝統的な装飾が施されている
5. 北側カーブサイド
6. 国際線，国内線両ターミナルを結ぶコリドー内に設けられた中庭
7. 中央プラザから割れ門越しにエアサイドを見る
4. A corridor of the international terminal
5. View of the curbside from the west
6. A courtyard between domestic and international terminal
7. View of the airside from the central plaza

8. 国際線ターミナル・東側ビルのレストランエリア
9. コンセッションエリアとその中央ラウンジ席
10. チェックインカウンターを経て2階デパーチャー
    ラウンジへ至る階段。ここにもバリ・ヒンズーか
    ら引用された石彫や装飾が随所に見られる
8. Restaurant and concession area on upper
   level in the international terminal
9. Concession and lounge area on upper
   level in the international terminal
10. View of the stairs leading to departure lounge (2F)

9

10

11

●観光リゾートの成長とともに急速に伸び続ける空港需要

バリ・ヌグアライ国際空港は、多数の島々からなるインドネシアのほぼ中央、ジャワ島の東側に隣接する5569km²の小さな島、バリ島の南部に位置している。バリ島はこの10年で世界的な観光リゾートとして脚光を浴びているが、その中心的な観光エリアであるクタ、サヌール、ヌサドゥアといったビーチに対してほぼ等距離にあり、車で約30分ほどでアクセスできる。1969年に国際空港として供用が始まって以来、バリを訪れる観光客の数は著しく増加した。それにともない、バリ・ヌグアライ国際空港の需要も急激に伸び、1987年にはスラバヤ空港を抜いて、首都のジャカルタ空港に次ぐインドネシア第2の空港に成長してきた。1980年代初期の世界的に航空需要が低迷した時期においても、バリ・ヌグアライ国際空港の需要は伸び続け、1994年には年間旅客数は430万人に達している。空港需要の増加にともない、空港の諸施設は適宜拡張、整備されてきたが、さらに高まる空港需要に対応し、国際的水準での空港施設の完備、サービスの提供を促進するため、インドネシア政府は日本政府に技術協力を求め、空港整備のためのマスタープランが策定された。日本の海外経済協力基金（OECF）の財政協力および日本の設計

チームの技術協力のもと、新設された国際線ターミナル施設を含む第1次空港整備プロジェクトが、1992年に完成した。

●伝統的なバリの思想が表現されたターミナル

旅客ターミナルビルは国際線2万9900m²、国内線9500m²の面積を持つ両ターミナルで構成されている。外装およびインテリアは、多様なバリの伝統的デザインで統一され、ターミナル内の各所に配された現地のマテリアルを使った職人の手になる装飾が、バリのローカル・アイデンティティーを感じさせ、旅客の目を楽しませている。特に国際線ターミナルのカーブサイド側中央部に設けられたフェスティバル・プラザは、伝統的なバリの思想を表現したもので、ここは公務上や観光上の目的で伝統舞踊やセレモニーが披露される場となっている。また到着通路のブリッジをはさんだエアサイド側にはバリの寺院建築を引用した割れ門が設けられ、バリと外界を結ぶ象徴的な存在となっている。1992年の第一次開発プロジェクト終了以来、特に国際線ターミナルのコンセッション施設の充実が図られ、1994年現在で、3560m²に108のテナントが営業している。

●進む第2次開発プロジェクト

航空需要の増加は21世紀中期まで上昇を続けるという予測がなされており、バリ・ヌグアライ国際空港も2018年には2000万人の年間旅客数に対応できるような空港施設の拡張が要求されている。同時に、周囲の自然環境や社会環境を破壊しない開発のアセスメント、プランニングが必要となってきている。現在、バリ空港では、将来の空港拡張の必要性、バリの観光事業に起因する自然・文化の特殊性、急成長を続ける旅客数の増加率などを見据えた第二次開発プロジェクトが、1998年完成をめどに進行中である。これは年間旅客数950万人（国際線610万人、国内線340万人）に至るまでの対応が目指されている。

11. 国際線ターミナル1階のチェックインカウンター
11. Check-in counters on the ground level of the inetrnational terminal

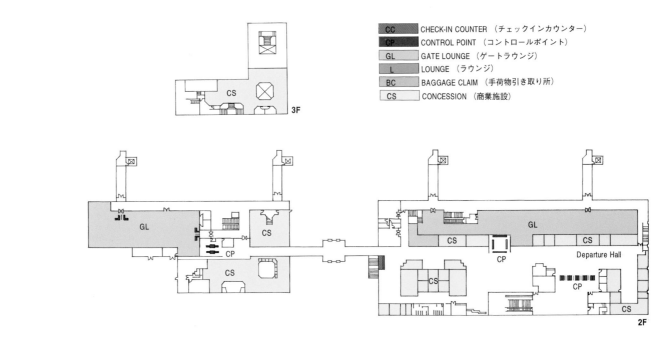

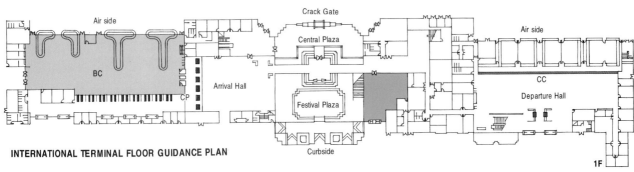

INTERNATIONAL TERMINAL FLOOR GUIDANCE PLAN

● RAPIDLY GROWING RESORT
DESTINATION

Ngurah Rai Bali International Airport is located in the southern part of Bali, a small island with an area of 5,569 square kilometers. Bali in turn is located in the center of Indonesia and adjacent to the island of Java. The Bali has gained worldwide popularity as a resort destination. From the airport, resort travelers can reach any of the main beaches—Kuta, Sanur and Nusa Dua—in 30 minutes by car.

Since the airport started international service in 1969, visitors to Bali have increased markedly. By 1987, the airport had become the second most popular in the nation after Jakarta International—passing Surabaya Airport. Even in the period of worldwide economic stagnancy in the early 1980s, demand continuously increased, reaching 4.3 million passengers in 1994.

To meet this demand, the airport facilities have been expanding, and the government has requested technical cooperation from the Japanese government for upgrading the airport, to provide an international level of service. With the cooperation of Japan's Overseas Economic Cooperation Fund (OECF) and a Japanese engineering design team in financial and technical matters, respectively, the Phase I Development Project, including international terminal facilities, was completed in 1992.

● TERMINAL EXPRESSES BALINESE
PHILOSOPHY

The terminal is composed of the international building, with 29,900 square meters of floor space, and the domestic building, which has 9,500 square meters.

Exterior and interior designs are integrated with various Balinese traditional decorations and local materials. Highlight is the Festival Plaza at the center of the international terminal which hosts traditional dances and ceremonies. On the airside of the arrival bridges, a temple gate, echoing Bali's typical Hindu temple architecture, attracts people's eyes as a symbol connecting Bali and the rest of the world.

Since the completion of Phase I in 1992, concessions at the international terminal have improved. As of 1994, 3,500 square meters was being used by 108 concessionaires.

● AIRPORT DEVELOPMENT PROJECT,
PHASE II

Demand is expected to increase steadily through the mid-21st century. To serve the 20 million passengers per year expected by 2018, the airport's capacity must be expanded. This process will include due consideration for the natural and social environment, as well as emphasis on the unique Balinese culture.

The first part of this process is Phase II, which should be completed in 1998. The expansion will give the airport the capacity to handle up to 9.5 million passengers per year—6.1 million international passengers and 3.4 million domestic passengers.

Text and Data Contributor
IR.Yayoen Wahyoe
Director of Operation
PT(Persero)Angkasa Pura I
Ngurah Rai/Bali International Airport

「フロリダ」をテーマとした美とテクノロジーのショーケース

オーランド国際空港

アメリカ，フロリダ州，オーランド

ORLANDO INTERNATIONAL AIRPORT

Orlando, Florida, USA

1. メーンターミナルビルの南側（ランドサイドB）カーブサイド
2. エアサイドターミナル（サテライトB）から見たコントロールタワーとメーンターミナルビル
3. メーンターミナルビル屋上から西側のコントロールタワーとエアサイドターミナル（サテライトA，B）方向を見る
1. View of the main terminal from the south side parking building
2. View of the main terminal and control tower from the satellite B
3. View of the satellite A and B (west side) from the main terminal top garage

1

2

3

5

6

4. エアサイドターミナル（サテライトC）の中央ホール。「フロリダ」をテーマに陽光と緑にあふれた空間となっている
5、6. エアサイドターミナル（サテライトC）の中央プラザから延びるボーディングゲートとそのラウンジまわり
7. エアサイドターミナル（サテライトC）側のAGTシステム（シャトルトレイン）駅
8. エアサイドターミナル（サテライトA）側のAGTシステム（シャトルトレイン）駅
4. The center hall of the airside terminal (satellite C)
5. 6. Boarding lounge of the airside terminal (satellite C)
7. The station of AGT shuttle train in the airside terminal (satellite C)
8. The station of AGT shuttle train in the airside terminal (satellite A)

7

8

9

9. メーンターミナルビル内のエアポート・ホテル（センチュリー・ハイアット）のアトリウム空間
   "パーク・ライク"をテーマに各所に設けられた噴水や植栽が天井トップライトから降り注ぐ陽光に照らされ，フロリダらしさを演出している
10. ジャングルのように多様な亜熱帯植物が生い茂ったパーキングビル
9. View of the airport hotel atrium in the main terminal
10. View of the south side parking building

11

12

13

●世界有数のリゾート王国への玄関口

オーランド国際空港はフロリダ半島のほぼ中央に位置する、世界でも有数の観光リゾートタウン・オーランドの市街地から約13kmという至近距離にある。ウォルト・ディズニー・ワールド、ユニバーサル・スタジオ、シーワールドといったテーマパークや、ケネディ宇宙センターやデイトナ・ビーチなど多彩な観光スポットへの玄関口として、アメリカ国内だけでなく世界中の旅客から人気の高い空港である。

オーランド空港は、70年以上にわたり、フロリダの航空史において指導的役目を担ってきている。1975年の空軍基地の閉鎖により、政府から市当局にこの土地の権利が譲渡された時から、オーランド国際空港の商業空港としての歴史が始まった。1981年には年間旅客数600万人に対応できるメーンターミナルビルと二つのエアサイドターミナルが完成し、その後、年々増えつづける旅客需要に対応するため、ターミナルビル、エアフィールド、テナント区域などの改築拡張が行われてきた。さらに1990年には新しく24ゲートある第三のエアサイドターミナルがオープンし、ほぼ現在の施設構成に至っている。これにより、1975年には約350万人だった年間総旅客数も、1994年には2240万人を数えるまでになっている。旅客の大半は、この空港を目的地としており、典型的なOD空港（Origination & Destination）である。

●フロリダのローカリティーとアメニティを表現

オーランド国際空港は、フロリダをテーマとし、"美とテクノロジーのショーケース"というコンセプトに設計の基準が置かれている。空港敷地中央に配された850エーカー（約350万m²）にもおよぶターミナル・サイトは亜熱帯の緑に覆われ、湖や島が点在する美しい景観が大切に保護されている。また、ユニークな建築スタイルを持つモダンなターミナル・コンプレックスも、みずみずしい熱帯の風景から生まれたように周囲の景観と違和感なくマッチし、ここを訪れる旅客にフロリダの環境とその自然の豊かさと美しさを感じさせる。オーランド空港は周囲の環境との協調において、世界で最も先進的な空港である。空港ターミナルビルは、ランドサイド側のメーンターミナルと、そこから放射状に延びる三つのエアサイドターミナルから構成されており、その総規模は約46万5000m²にもおよぶが、メーンターミナルと各エアサイドターミナル間を、AGTシステム（シャトルトレイン）で結ぶことにより、搭乗ゲートまでの歩行距離は最長でも約260m以内におさめられている。同時に搭乗旅客は、一度も上下移動することなくメーンターミナルから搭乗ゲートにアクセスすることができる。1992年8月には、メーンターミナル内にハイアット・ホテル＆リゾートの運営による全447室を持つエアポートホテルがオープンした。このホテルとターミナルとを結ぶアトリウム空間は、"Park-like"をテーマに設計され、噴水や植栽を天井開口部から差し込む陽光が照らしだし、「フロリダ」らしさを盛り上げている。ターミナル内には、エアラインやコンセッション施設を含め約170のテナントが入居しているが、多様な飲食施設のほか、ディズニー・ワールドやユニバーサル・スタジオなどのキャラクターグッズ・ショップがやはりフロリダらしさの演出の一つとなっている。現在は、さらなる空港需要の増加に対応するため、第四のエアサイドターミナルの建設が進行中である。また、将来的な方向としては、観光産業への対応だけでなく、国際会議場やビジネスセンターとしてオーランドの成長を図るべく、また国際線の自由化に向けて積極的な活動を行っていく方針である。

11. メーンターミナルのコンセッションエリアには世界有数の観光リゾートタウン、オーランドが誇る様々なテーマパークのキャラクターショップが並ぶ。写真はディズニー・ワールドのショップ
12. ユニバーサル・スタジオのショップ
13. シーワールドのショップ
11. Theme park retail "Walt Disney World" in the main terminal(3F)
12. Theme park retail "Universal Studio of Florlda" (3F)
13. Theme park retail "Sea World" (3F)

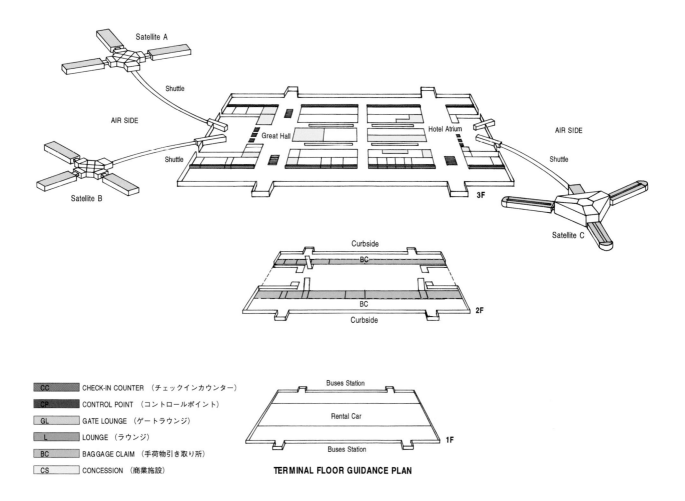

Satellite A

Shuttle

AIR SIDE

Great Hall

Hotel Atrium

AIR SIDE

Shuttle

Shuttle

Satellite B

3F

Satellite C

Curbside

BC

BC

2F

Curbside

CC CHECK-IN COUNTER （チェックインカウンター）

CP CONTROL POINT （コントロールポイント）

GL GATE LOUNGE （ゲートラウンジ）

L LOUNGE （ラウンジ）

BC BAGGAGE CLAIM （手荷物引き取り所）

CS CONCESSION （商業施設）

Buses Station

Rental Car

1F

Buses Station

TERMINAL FLOOR GUIDANCE PLAN

●GATEWAY TO THE WORLD'S FOREMOST RESORT KINGDOM

Orlando International Airport is located only 13 kilometers from downtown Orlando, a world-renowned resort town situated in the center of the Florida peninsula. Serving as a gateway to the various tourist attractions—Walt Disney World, Universal Studios, Sea World, the Kennedy Space Center and Daytona Beach—the airport attracts passengers from the United States and around the globe.

Orlando has played a leading role in Florida's aviation history for more than 70 years. Orlando International Airport started commercial operations in 1975 when the U.S. Government transferred the property to the City of Orlando after the closure of an air force base.

In 1981, a new terminal complex opened. It was composed of a main terminal and two airside terminal buildings accommodating 6 million passengers per year. Since then the terminal complex, air field and concession area have been improved and expanded to meet continuously increasing demand. The terminal complex was expanded a second time in 1990 with the opening of a new 24 gates—third airside terminal. This expansion completed the present terminal's form—a

main landside terminal and three airside terminal buildings. The airport handled more than 22.4 million passengers in 1994, compared with 3.5 million in 1975 when commercial operations began. The airport is predominantly an origination and destination (O&D) airport with a relatively small percentage of passengers making connections.

●EXPRESSING LOCAL COLOR AND HOSPITALITY

Orlando International Airport is considered an aesthetic and technological showcase for its designs based on Florida themes. The terminal site occupies approximately 3.5 million square meters (850 acres) of carefully preserved natural land, dotted with lakes and islands. The unique architectural style of the modern complex seems to grow out of the lush, tropical landscape, providing a good contrast with the natural surroundings and accenting the characteristic environment, nature and beauty of Florida. Orlando International was the first airport in the world to adopt the beauty of the natural environment in the airport development process.

The airport terminal complex is composed of a main terminal on the landside and three airside terminal buildings arrayed radially around the main terminal. In spite of its large

total area of 465,000 square meters, passengers' walking distance to boarding gates is limited to approximately 260 meters, as all buildings are linked by the AGT system shuttle trains. Passengers reach the gates from the main terminal without any vertical movement.

In August 1992, an airport hotel, managed by Hyatt Corporation, opened in the main terminal. It features a park-like atrium, connecting the hotel and the terminal. The fountains and plants are naturally lit through the roof light and express Florida's characteristic environment. About 170 concessionaires operate in the terminal, offering not only food and beverages, but also retail goods from Disney World and Universal Studios.

To meet further increases in demand, construction of the fourth airside terminal building is underway. With Orlando's growth as a business center, the airport's management expects future demand to come from conventions and other business-related travel, along with the tourist trade. Liberalization of international air travel should also boost demand.

Text and Data Contributor
Carolyn M.Fennell
Director of Community Relations
Orlando International Airport

ニース・コートダジュール空港

フランス，ニース

NICE COTE D'AZUR AIRPORT

Nice, France

1. 旅客機への乗降口であるボーディング・ブリッジよりターミナル2を見る
2. 地中海を背に滑走路越しにターミナル1を見る。コートダジュール（紺碧海岸）の中心となる空港である
3. アプローチ道路よりターミナル1を見る。駐車場には温暖な気候の地らしく常緑の樹木が数多く植栽されている
1. View of the terminal 2 from the boarding bridge
2. View of the terminal 1 and runway from airside
3. View of the terminal 1 from an approach road

1

2

4

5

4. ターミナル1のカーブサイド。上部の外通路は非常用で普段は使われない
5. ターミナル2の出発フロア（2階レベル）カーブサイド
6. ターミナル2のエアサイドよりガラスとトラス構造のボーディング・ブリッジを見る
7. 旅客機へと続くボーディング・ブリッジ。その向こう側には地中海が広がる

4. Curbside of the terminal 1
5. Curbside of the terminal 2
6. View of the boarding bridge from airside
7. The boarding bridge in the terminal 2

6

7

9

10

8. ターミナル1の1階中央吹き抜けアトリウム
9. ターミナル2の2階ゲートラウンジ。左上のガラス開口部は自動開閉式のルーバーである
10. ターミナル1の2階ゲートラウンジ。ガラス張りになった3階にはレストランとビジネスラウンジが並ぶ
8. View of the atrium in the terminal 1(1F)
9. View of the gate lounge in the terminal 2(2F)
10. View of the gate lounge in the terminal 1(2F)

8

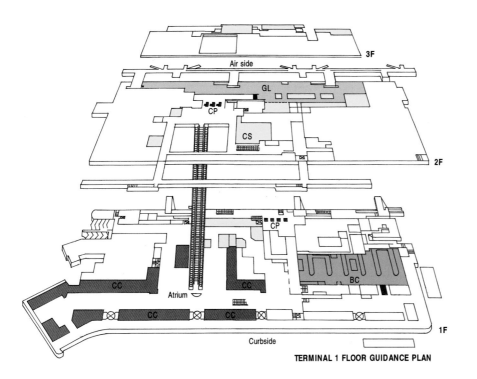

TERMINAL 1 FLOOR GUIDANCE PLAN

3F
Air side
GL
CP
CS
2F

CC
CC
Atrium
BC
CC
CC
CC
CC
Curbside
1F

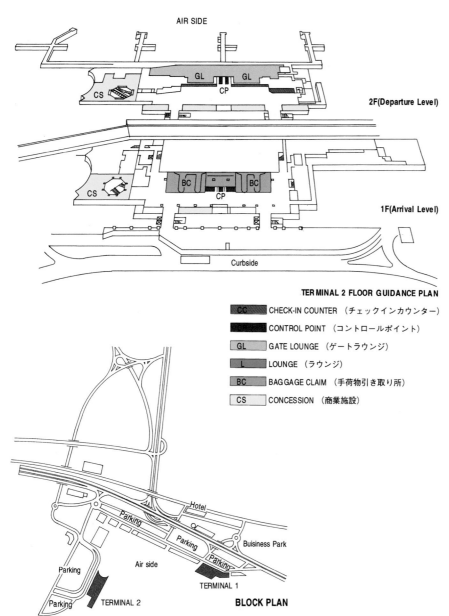

AIR SIDE

GL GL
CS CP
2F(Departure Level)

CS BC BC
CP
1F(Arrival Level)

Curbside

TERMINAL 2 FLOOR GUIDANCE PLAN

CC	CHECK-IN COUNTER （チェックインカウンター）
CP	CONTROL POINT （コントロールポイント）
GL	GATE LOUNGE （ゲートラウンジ）
L	LOUNGE （ラウンジ）
BC	BAGGAGE CLAIM （手荷物引き取り所）
CS	CONCESSION （商業施設）

Hotel
Parking
Parking
Parking
Buisiness Park
Parking
Air side
Parking
TERMINAL 1
TERMINAL 2
BLOCK PLAN

●サンベルトの中心に位置

ヨーロッパ経済の引力の中心は，今やハイテク産業，高付加価値活動，高度教育，リサーチ，各種会議，経済および企業サービスが集中する，南の"サンベルト"に移行しつつある。このサンベルトと呼ばれる陽光地帯の特色は，若く外向的な住民，高水準な生活，クオリティ・オブ・ライフ，成長と成功，などに表されている。ニース・コートダジュール空港は，まさにこのサンベルトの中心に位置し，南ヨーロッパへ広がる東西の中枢をなしている。また，世界主要都市へのフライトはヨーロッパ45便，北米1便，その他の都市12便を含む計91便が運行されている。1994年の国際線旅客部門売り上げ率は5％の伸びを示し，そのパフォーマンスはマンチェスター，ミュンヘン，ミラノのような主要ユーロポートと肩を並べるようになった。特に北米市場は，14万人もの大西洋横断旅客数を運び，成功を収めている。地元リビエラ市場は，マルセイユからイタリアのトリノまで1000万人以上の消費人口を擁し，その市場の60％はイタリアにある。

●ビジネス利用とレジャー利用は50対50

リビエラは自然美の宝庫である。美しい立地，温暖な気候，そして素晴らしい環境に恵まれている。そのため，ここリビエラはリゾート，観光地というイメージが強いが，実際はこの数十年の間に，ハイテク産業からも多くの収入を上げるようになってきた。現在では，ニース・コートダジュール空港の運行量はビジネスとレジャーは50対50の同比を示しており，年間を通じて見るとビジネス旅客が優勢を示している。44エアラインの乗り入れにより，1994年には620万人の旅客数を記録したこの空港では，引き続きビジネス旅客の増加に力を注いでいく予定である。

●ブルースカイアプローチ

この空港では，霧はなく，雪もなく，渋滞もないという完璧な運行状況で，フライトの75％が時間通りに発着している。1992年には新しいATCタワーも開設され，6000万ドルを投じた国際線旅客ターミナル（ターミナル2）の改修工事の完成を見た。これには新出発区域および，共通利用のビジネスラウンジ「クラブ・リビエラ」も含まれている。このターミナル設計においては，観光地として名高いこの南仏の陽の恵みや緑が積極的に取り入れられており，例えば，ガラス開口部などには自動開閉式ルーバーを採用したり，駐車場やブリッジ通路などにはグリーンを意識的に配置することで空港利用客にやすらぎを与える結果となっている。これら空港事業は質的にも量的にも2010年までにさらに充実され，その完成時にはニース・コートダジュール空港は年間1200万人の旅客の受け入れが可能となる。将来的には，南ヨーロッパへのゲートウエーとしてのニース開発，欧州ネットワークの統合，アメリカおよび極東への年間を通じての連結機能の開発などの目標が掲げられている。

11. ターミナル1の3階にあるビジネスセンター
11. View of the business center in the terminal 1(3F)

11

●THE HEART OF THE SUNBELT

Europe's economic center of gravity is moving south to the Sunbelt, a concentrated area of high-tech industry, high-value-added activity, higher education, research, congresses, financial and corporate services. The Sunbelt is characterized by a young and outgoing population, a high standard of living and quality of life, growth and success. Nice Côte d'Azur Airport lies at the very heart of Europe's Sunbelt and is perfectly located to expand as an East-West hub to southern Europe. The airport has scheduled flights to 91 major cities worldwide: 45 flights to Europe, 1 flight to North America and 12 flights to the rest of the world.

In 1994, Nice-Riviera's international passenger business grew 5%, boosting the airport into the ranks of such major Euroports as Manchester, Munich and Milan. Demand related to the North American market has been particularly strong —140,000 transatlantic passengers in 1994. Nice-Riviera's regional market, stretching from Marseilles, France to Torino, Italy, has more than 10 million consumers. 60% of this market is in Italy.

●BUSINESS AND LEISURE PASSENGERS EQUAL IN NUMBER

The Riviera is a region with natural charms— beautiful locations, a mild climate and an exceptional environment. People often envision the Riviera as entirely resort, but the region's income from high-tech-related business has increased during the past few decades. Nice Côte d'Azur Airport's traffic is now half business and half leisure, and business passengers use the airport more regularly year-round. The airport handled 6.2 million passengers and 44 airlines in 1994 and will continue to attract more business passengers.

●THE BLUE SKY APPROACH

No fog, no snow, no congestion—rather, blue sky and sea characterize Nice Côte d'Azur Airport. With such perfect operating conditions, 75% of flights are on time. In 1992, the airport celebrated the inauguration of the new ATC tower and improvement of the international passenger terminal.These projects required $60 million. The terminal includes a new departure area and a business lounge, the Club Riviera. The terminal's design reflects the regional features of southern France by using sunlight and green plants. Automatic louvers on windows maximize natural light, and nicely arranged green plants in the parking facilities and elevated passages provide travelers comfort and relaxation.

Nice Côte d'Azur Airport will improve in quality and in capacity by the year 2010, when 12 million passengers per year are expected. Plans are targeted at three goals:establishing Nice as the gateway to Southern Europe, consolidating the already solid European network and creating year-round links to North America and the Far East.

Text and Data Contributor
Benoît Aonzo
Chairman
Aéroports Nice Côte d'Azur

エコロジカル・アイランドづくりを目指すミニ都市としての海上空港

関西国際空港

大阪府泉佐野市

KANSAI INTERNATIONAL AIRPORT

Izumisano, Osaka, Japan

1. 関西空港駅側からブリッジ越しに新設された商業施設棟・エアロプラザの西側正面ファサードを見る
2. 南側から見た空港ターミナルの航空写真。左右に翼を広げたような全体フォルムがよく分かる
3. エアロプラザ11階のスカイラウンジ「ジェットストリーム」内部客席より窓側開口部越しに旅客ターミナルの大屋根を見る
1. View of Aero Plaza from the railroad station
2. Birds-eye view of the airport terminal from the south side
3. View from the sky lounge in Aero Plaza(11F) to the airport terminal

4

5

4. 旅客ターミナル4階の国際線出発フロア。天井のオープンダクトが空間を特徴づけている
5. 旅客ターミナル2階のゲートラウンジからエアサイドのフィンガーを見る
6. 旅客ターミナルのカーブサイド側に設けられたキャニオンを2階レベルから見る。空間自体が巨大なサインとなっている

4. View of the international departure floor in the airport terminal(4F)
5. View from the gate lounge in the airport terminal(2F) to air side
6. Whole view of the canyon from the second floor level

6

8

9

7. 商業棟・エアロプラザ2階のホテルとショッピングゾーンを分ける巨大なアトリウムを3階レベルから見る
8. エアロプラザの大部分を占める「ホテル関西空港」の2階レストラン「ザ・ブラッスリー」内部客席
9. エアロプラザ1階に配された「ホテル関西空港」のフロントロビーまわり
10. ホテル2階の天ぷら「花ざと」カウンター席
11. 同じくホテル2階の中国料理「桃李」円形テーブル席
7. Whole view of the atrium in Aero Plaza from the third floor level
8. View of the restaurant in the hotel(2F)
9. View of the reception and lobby in the hotel(1F)
10. View of the tempura restaurant in the hotel(2F)
11. View of the chinese restaurant in the hotel(2F)

10

11

●エコロジカル・アイランド
関西国際空港は，大阪湾に浮かぶ総面積510ha，3500mの滑走路1本を有する海上空港である。沖合4km，水深18mのところに，1億5000万m³の土砂を埋め立て，造成されたこの空港は人工島のため，騒音が陸上におよばないことから夢の空港といわれており，日本初の24時間運用で，アジアのハブ空港を目指し，1994年9月に開港した。構想から四半世紀，1兆5000億円の巨費を投じた国家的プロジェクトであった。現在，世界28カ国と結ばれ，国際線の便数は週459便。高速道路2系列と鉄道，高速船が直結する多様なアクセスが魅力となっている。ちなみに航空燃料も大型タンカーで海上を運ばれる。ターミナルビルは，4階の国際線出発フロアと1階の国際線到着フロアが，2階の国内線を挟む「サンドイッチ構造」になっている。そのため国際線と国内線の乗り継ぎは，エスカレーターやエレベーターの上下移動だけで簡単にでき，また国際線の各ゲートへの移動は，快適でスピーディ

ーなウイングシャトルでスムーズにできる。このコンセプトは，パリ空港公団ポール・アンドリューの提案によるものである。また，国際コンペにより選ばれた，レンゾ・ピアノの設計になるターミナルビルは，ハイテクと自然が融合する斬新なデザインで高い評価を受けている。空港駅からターミナルビルに入ると，「キャニオン」と呼ばれる巨大な吹き抜け空間が出迎える。旅客は自分の居場所やこれから行くべき場所を容易に認識することができる。ピアノは，ここを天然樹木と日本的なベンガラ色で演出，アメニティ豊かな「メディアスペース」として機能している。関西国際空港は，空港島の地区別に基本カラーとアクセントカラーの設定や，島内全域にわたって環境保全林（ワイルドグリーン）と庭園植栽（ガーデン）を計画的に配置するなどの景観コントロールが行われている。また，島の周囲の護岸には魚が住み，魚礁となっているなど，未来都市をイメージするエコロジカル・アイランドづくりへの試みも行われている。

●ユーザー・フレンドリーな空港
関西国際空港の基本となる経営目標は，「ユーザー・フレンドリーな空港」の実現にある。それを具体化する柱は次の五つである。
1．国際，国内の重要な拠点空港としての使命を達成すること。
2．旅客や利用者の利便性，快適性に十分配慮した施設運営やサービスを行うこと。
3．空港の安全の確保に万全を期すこと。
4．営業収入の最大限の確保に努め，企業経営の健全性の確保を図ること。
5．地域社会との共存共栄を図ること。
関西国際空港は，日本では初めての試みである株式会社による経営になる。そのため，開港後5年で単年度黒字，9年で累積損失の解消という，ハードな収支目標が課せられており，収入の拡大は大きな営業課題である。そのための方策として，ターミナル内の直営店舗の営業や複合商業施設のエアロプラザの運営，あるいは見学展望ホールなどの運営に力を入れている。現在，非航空収入の割合は約6割で，新東京国際空港が約2割であることから見ると，その努力は実りつつあると言える。

●都市化の核としてのエアロプラザ
旅客の多様なニーズに応え，最大限の満足を提供するユーザー・フレンドリーな空港と，非航空収入の拡大とは何ら矛盾しない。むしろ，相乗的な関係にある。その両方の目標を達成するために，1995年，都市機能を持ったエアロプラザが開発された。空港駅に隣接するエアロプラザは，高級ホテルやレストランゾーン，ショッピングゾーンなどからなる複合商業施設である。ターミナルビルの方にも高度な商業集積があるが，そちらは主にクイックの客に対応し，エアロプラザの方は主にステイの客に対応して，相互に補完的な機能を持っているのである。高級ホテルの客室数は576室，商業施設は2万m²，延べ床面積は6万3000m²におよぶ。ホテルの付属施設として，カラオケルーム，ゴルフシミュレーション，リフレッシュ施設，ビジネスセンターなど，多彩な利便施設を備えている。エアロプラザは空港の都市化に先鞭をつけるものであり，また地域との共生にも寄与するものである。また，将来計画としては，ホテルの増設や業務ビル建設の構想などがある。開港して1年あまり，空港の立地が刺激となって，大阪湾岸の関連産業や周辺プロジェクトも動き始めた。乗り入れ便数も旅客数も確実に増加している。現状の滑走路1本では増大する航空需要に追いつかず，早晩能力不足になることが予想されている。このため，現在3本の滑走路を有した全体構想の，早期実現が検討されている。

Air side
North Wing　　MAIN TERMINAL　　South Wing

4F

3F
Wing Shuttle　　L　　Wing Shuttle
CS
Canyon

2F
Air side
GL
BC
Canyon

1F
BC
Canyon
Curbside
MAIN TERMINAL FLOOR GUIDANCE PLAN

CC	CHECK-IN COUNTER	（チェックインカウンター）
CP	CONTROL POINT	（コントロールポイント）
GL	GATE LOUNGE	（ゲートラウンジ）
L	LOUNGE	（ラウンジ）
BC	BAGGAGE CLAIM	（手荷物引き取り所）
CS	CONCESSION	（商業施設）

12．神戸との海上アクセス基地である水中翼船用ターミナル内部の待合スペース
13．北側から見た空港全景。海に浮かぶ人工島であることがよく分かる
12．Interior view of the hydrofoil terminal
13．Birds-eye view of the airport from the north

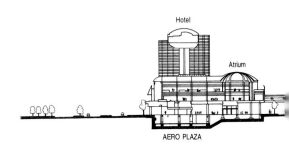

Hotel
Atrium
AERO PLAZA

12

13

● AN ECOLOGICAL ISLAND

Kansai International Airport is a sea airport, seemingly afloat in Osaka Bay, with a total area of 510 hectares and a 3,500-meter runway. The airport was inaugurated in September 1994 as Japan's first to operate around the clock, and it is expected to become a bustling Asian hub. It is one of the country's largest construction projects to date, requiring ¥1.5 trillion (about US$15 billion) and 25 years from initial planning to completion.

The airport island rises from a depth of 18 meters and is composed of 180 million cubic meters of earth and sand. Since it is located four kilometers offshore, most of the airport's noise does not reach the mainland. Without noise pollution, it can be used around The clock.

Kansai International handles 459 flights weekly to and from 28 countries. Two expressways, a rail line and a high-speed sea shuttle serve the airport, and aviation fuel is delivered by large tankers.

The four-story terminal has its domestic service on the second floor, sandwiched between international arrivals on the first floor and international departures on the fourth floor. Concessions and shuttle train service are on the third floor. Escalators and elevators easily transport passengers between the domestic and internationa floors, and the comfortable and speedy Wing Shuttle gets them to their gates. These concepts were proposed by Paul Andrew of A roports de Paris.

The terminal building's design, by Renzo Piano, has won an international award and high acclaim for its blending of high technolo-gy and nature. At the entrance, a huge empty space called the Canyon welcomes visitors and allows them to see their way easily. Piano's design for the entrance features natural trees and a brick-red color scheme, which are used to create a Japanese motif. The entrance functions as a "media space", offering a variety of amenities.

The island is not only functional but also aesthetically and ecologically appealing as basic and accent colors are designated area by area, and wild greens and gardens are arranged pleasingly. The seawalls of the airport island have became man-made reefs attracting shoals of fish : an attempt toward an ecological island.

●USER-FRIENDLY AIRPORT

Kansai International's management strives to make it truly user-friendly. The airport's five basic operating goals are:
1. To become an important international and domestic hub airport
2. To provide top-quality service, comfort and convenience
3. To maintain safety
4. To secure maximum profit to achieve sound management
5. To coexist with the surrounding communi-ties for mutual benefits

Because it is Japan's first airport operated by a private corporation, management has set stringent revenue and expenditure goals. These include operating in the black by the fifth fiscal year from its opening, and a complete paydown of the accumulated debt by the ninth. To boost non-aviation revenue, management also operates some of the concessions, such as the Aero Plaza and the visitors' observation hall. Non-aviation revenue is currently 60%, while New Tokyo International Airport's figure is 20%.

● AERO PLAZA AS A NUCLEUS OF URBANIZATION

Kansai International's high ratio of non-aviation revenue in the total revenue is an expression of management's effort to create a user-friendly airport by meeting various passenger needs and providing maximum satisfaction. Aero Plaza, a commercial complex opened in 1995, offers an example. The facility features a high-class hotel, restaurants and shopping areas. Aero Plaza is designed primarily for the use of people with plenty of time to spend, while other commercial facilities in the main terminal building serve people with less time. Thus they are mutually complementary.

The hotel has a total area of 63,000 square meters, including 20,000 square meters of commercial area, and 576 guest rooms. Among the amenities are *karaoke*, virtual golf, foods and beverages and a business center. Aero Plaza is a forerunner of airport urbanization. Management plans to develop more hotels and commercial facilities.

The business environment in the Osaka metropolitan area has received a boost since the airport's opening. As the number of flights increase, the runway's capacity will soon be reached. Thus management is reviewing its expansion plans, aiming at three runways in total.

Text and Data Contributor
Yoichi Arai

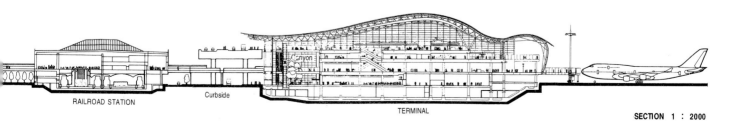

RAILROAD STATION   Curbside   TERMINAL   **SECTION 1 : 2000**

ヒューマン・エアポートのエレメント ——————————— 新井洋一

人間性を基調とした新しい空港，新世代空港の施設や空間をどうとらえ，計画していったらいいのだろうか。ここではソフトに対するハードという意味で，新世代空港の空間のデザインエレメントを特徴的なキーワードに基づき，まとめてみよう。

概括的に新世代空港を特徴づけているのは，「都市化の進展」である。空港はいま多くの都市的機能を取り込み，より複合化を進め，都市的規模の商業施設としての特性を強めつつある。そこで，新たな動きとして出てきたのが，開放された大空間による多機能の統合と融合であろう。

スキポール空港は「ワンルーフ・コンセプト（一つ屋根の下にすべての施設がある）」を特徴の一つとし，フランクフルト空港も「全てのサービスを一つ屋根の下で」得られることを基本理念にしている。オープンしたばかりのスキポール空港の「プラザ」は，複合ショッピングセンターと国鉄駅を組み込んだ空間で，「一つ屋根の下」の考え方を大胆に具現化したものだ。ガラスと鉄骨の大きな屋根の架構，光が降り注ぐ開放感あふれるアトリウムは，「一つ屋根の下」の空間の象徴的な形である。関西国際空港は，ターミナルビルの入り口に，キャニオンと呼ばれる幅300m，奥行き25m，高さ25mの巨大な吹き抜け空間を設けている。自然光とガラスを多用した見通しのある広大な空間は，いま多くの空港で共通の風景となった。

これらは，かつて街路に天蓋を架けて都市の外部空間を内部化した，ミラノのガレリアの現代版といえるかもしれない。外部空間が大屋根で覆われることによって，単なる通路が開放され

デンバー国際空港メーンターミナル

ELEMENTES OF HUMAN AIRPORT　　Text by Yoichi Arai

The airport of the new generation is people-oriented. How should the hardware—the space and facilities—of the new-generation airport be conceptualized and planned? What are the design elements of the new human airport?

It may be noted that "urbanization" is the concept that characterizes the new-generation airport. Airports in the world have become equipped more and more with urban functions, complexty and large-scale commercial outlets. A new solution to integrate these urban facilities is a huge open space under "one roof."

The "one-roof" concept (All facilities under one roof) characterizes Amsterdam Schiphol Airport while one of Frankfurt Ariport's basic principles is "All service under one roof." The brand-new Schiphol Plaza is a daring realization of the "one-roof" concept, combining a complex shopping center and the national railway station. The glass-and-steel structure of the huge roof and the sunshining open atrium are the symbols of the "one-roof" space. Kansai International Airport has a "Canyon" at the entrance of the terminal building. It is a huge atrium of 300m in width, 25m in depth and 25m in height. A large open space with natural light through wide glass walls has become a common sight in many of the world's airports. It may be regarded as a modern version of Milan's Galleria, where the street was covered by a canopy and turned into an interior space. A mere street had been transformed into a "media space" or "communication space" where people leisurely walked around and met friends. People did not just walk through it. The new airports are now beginning to have a "media space" with integrated open atmosphere with multiple functions. The openness and spaciousness have changed a cold and

た内部空間として，人々が相互に認識し合うメディアスペース，交流空間へと変貌した。人々はここを単に通過するだけではなく，回遊し交流する楽しみを発見した。巨大空港もまさに，多種多様なファンクションを一つ屋根の下にまとめて，「メディアスペース」により一体性と開放性を持ってきているといえよう。開放された大空間が飛行機の乗降のための無機質な場を交流とにぎわいの場に変えた。人々は勝手知った街のように，やわらかく動き，店をのぞき，ベンチで憩い，体験を共有し，ひとときを楽しむ。新世代空港は，「メディアスペース」としての新たな交流空間を伴って，その姿を現しつつある。

新世代空港の空間を構成するエレメントを，わたしは次の八つのカテゴリーに分けてみた。

[1] ツーリング・イノベーション，[2] アミューズメント，[3] ビジネス・サポート，[4] アメニティ，[5] ローカル・アイデンティティ，[6] モビリティ，[7] ホスピタリティ，[8] コミュニケーション

これらを大きくくくると，次の三つの特性に分けられよう。

（A）アーバン・ミックス
旅客の多様化するニーズに応えるためのより多様な商業・ビジネス関係の施設………[1], [2], [3]
（B）ハイ・アメニティ
安全で心地よく周辺と調和のとれた環境整備………[4], [5]
（C）ハイ・モビリティ
空港本来の機能にかかわる，分かりやすくスムーズな動線確保………[6], [7], [8]

「アーバン・ミックス」「ハイ・アメニティ」「ハイ・モビリティ」，この三つの特性は，いずれも商業的に成功をめざす空港にとって，備えなくてはならない必須の課題であり，これを実現した空港が空港間競争に一歩先んずることができるのである。

（A）アーバン・ミックス
旅客のニーズの多様化への対応は，非航空収入の拡大を目指す世界の空港の経営方針の大きな柱となっている。多種多様な物

関西国際空港ターミナルの吹き抜けスペース「キャニオン」

functional place for air travel into a space of lively human contact. There, people feel at home and move with ease, stopping by a shop or resting on a bench. They relax and enjoy themselves, sharing experiences. Thus, the new-generation airport now emerges with a "media space", a space with new human qualities.

The elements that characterize the "human airport" may be classified into eight categories: 1-touring innovation, 2-amusement, 3-business support, 4-amenity, 5-local identity, 6-mobility, 7-hospitality and 8-communication. These eight items form three groups.

(A)Urban Mixture—Multi-functional commercial and business facilities to meet various passenger needs(1-2-3)
(B)High Amenity—Safe and comfortable environment that is harmonious with surroundings(4-5)
(C)High Mobility—Easy access and smooth movement to ensure basic funcutions of the airport(6-7-8)

Urban Mixture, High Amenity and High Mobility are the essential features of the airport which aspires to gain commercial success. An airport that achieves these goals takes the lead in the competition among world's airports.

(A)Urban Mixture
To increase non-aviation revenue, the airport management finds it important to meet various passenger needs. It is essential to line up profitable duty-free shops, various retail stores, foods and beverages and hotels. In Schiphol Airport, for example, the duty-free shopping center has more than 120,000 items for sale in its 45 shops. Upgraded amusement facilities of various types are also available.

One recent trend is that the airport management is shifting its business target from tourists to business people. Many airports are now opening full-scale business centers.

販店，飲食店，ホテルなどは必須のアイテムとなっている。スキポール空港の45のショップが揃ったショッピングセンターは総販売品目12万点を超える。さらに多様なお客のニーズに応えるための各種アミューズメントの施設の充実も試みられている。また，最近の動向として，多くの空港がターゲットを観光客からビジネス客へとシフトしつつある。本格的なビジネスセンターを空港内部に抱き込み始めた。
シャルル・ド・ゴール空港は空港の一角にビジネスセンターを，フランクフルト空港は旅客ターミナルに直結するビジネスゾーンをもち，空港を新たなビジネスの拠点にしようとしている。
（B）ハイ・アメニティ
空港は美しく清潔で，そして安全であることがより一層求められている。また，最近は，地域のランドマークとしての役割も重要視され，周辺の文化や景観や自然との調和・協調が要請されている。新たに建設されたミュンヘン空港や関西国際空港では，周辺環境との調和が開発の前提条件として取り

扱われた。関西国際空港は海上の沖合４kmの人工島のため騒音公害はなく，しかも島が魚礁の機能を果たしていて，沢山の魚の棲み家となっている。
（C）ハイ・モビリティ
スムーズで明快な動線，空港内の移動が便利なことは，空港の最も基本的で重要な要素である。空港機能の多様化にいかに努力しようとも，この要素に欠ける空港は空港として成立しない。旅客動線をより短く，より早く，より快適に。そのためエスカレータやエレベーターに加えて，動く歩道やＡＧＴなどハイテク設備が導入されている。また，空港と周辺の都市間の円滑な移動の確保も重要な要素である。最近は，鉄道と直結する空港が増えつつある。シャルル・ド・ゴール空港はフランスの高速新幹線ＴＧＶが空港に乗り入れ，ヨーロッパの交通の核としての位置づけが強まっている。空港母都市や他の都市へのアクセスの確保は，空港の競争力の大きな武器となっている。

フランクフルト空港第２ターミナルのチェックインカウンター

Charles de Gaulle Airport has a business center at a site of the terminal, while Frankfurt has a business zone directly connected to the passenger terminals. They try to provide a new base for business operations at the airport.

(B)High Amenity
Cleanliness, comfortableness and safety are always required at the airport. Also, the airport is being recognized as an important landmark of its region, and thus its design must be in harmony with the culture, landscape and nature of the area. In building Munich Airport and Kansai International Airport, the harmony with the surrounding enviroment was regarded a prerequisite.Locatecd on a reclaimed land four kilometers offshore, Kansai International Airport is free from noise pollution. Also note that the island's seawalls function as underwater reefs to attract abundant marine life.

(C)High Mobility
It is fundamentally important for the airport to provide smooth and convenient passenger movement. An airport cannot claim to be an airport without fulfilling this requirement. To achieve shorter, faster and more comfortable passenger movement, state-of-the-art facilities such as moving walkways and AGT(Automated Guideway Transit) System have been introduced in addition to escalators and elevators. Efficient linkage between the airport and neighboring cities is also a must. Recently, more and more airports get themselves directly connected to urban centers with railways. Charles de Gaulle Airport, for example, is becoming an important nucleus of European transportation network by bringing in French superexpress railway, the TGV. Easy access from an airport to its mother and surrounding cities is an essential element in its competitiveness.

空港はあたかも一流ホテルのロビーと最新ショッピングセンターがドッキングしたような形になりつつある。

〈ホテル〉ホテルは空港にとって必需の施設となってきている。オーランド空港のホテルは空港とホテルが結びついた典型であろう。コンコースを歩いていくと、いつのまにかホテルの中庭に出る。客室バルコニーがコンコースに面していて、空港を行き交う人々を眺めることができる。フランクフルト空港のホテルは最大規模を誇り、ターミナルビルと直結し、これもまた「一つ屋根の下」にある。ミュンヘン空港のホテルもコンコースに寄り添っており、大きな吹き抜けが旅客をもてなす。仮眠室的な、時間調整のための小さなホテルは昔からあったが、いまや空港のホテルはより大規模に、より本格的に、一流ホテルとしての内容を備えつつある。しかも、ターミナルビルと一体的に立地し始めている。ホテルでの滞在から既に旅は始まっている。その時間も旅のプロセスとして楽しみたいという旅客のニーズも大きくなっている。関西国際空港でも先頃、ターミナルビルに隣接して高級ホテルが開業した。四方を海で囲まれた、リゾ

1 ツーリング・イノベーション

Touring
Innovation

ートホテルのような趣に人気が集まっている。

〈レストラン〉滞在時間の長い空港では、飲食店は不可欠な施設である。「クイック」の、急ぎの客にはファストフード的なものを、「ステイ」の、ゆとりのある客には地域の特徴ある料理や高級レストランの味をと、旅客の動態に合わせた多様な業態が揃っている。市街地の高級レストランと遜色ない店も多く、空港利用客ばかりでなく、周辺地域の人々の需要にも応える傾向にな

っている。ミュンヘン空港も関西国際空港も、空港の見学と合わせて、飲食店を目当てに訪れる人も多い。チューリッヒ空港の「バイバイバー」はその名のごとく、乗り場の近くにあり、目の前に飛行機が見える。旅の気分に浸りながら、安心して、ひとときを楽しむことができる。コペンハーゲン空港にも飛行機を眼前にしたカフェがある。

〈物販〉空港でのショッピングは旅客にとって大きな楽しみの一つになってきている。最近は品揃え、価格の点で、市内の中心商店街と競合するほどのところが増えている。フランクフルト空港は、商業施設の多様化に先鞭をつけた空港だが、その集積は群を抜いている。スーパーマーケットまで揃え、周辺地域の人々までもが気軽に買物に訪れる。近年は第2ターミナル内に新たに商業コンプレックスを設けたり、旧ターミナルのリニューアルを図るなど、空港都市としての広がりは止まるところを知らない。また、免税売店の先鞭をつけたのはスキポール空港である。総販売品目12万点は他の追随を許さない。チャンギ空港は103もの小売店を擁し、市内と同じ値段を売り物にして、常に価格のモニターを怠らないという。

ミュンヘン空港内に新設された「ケンピンスキー・ホテル」の大アトリウム

スキポール空港の新設Gピアにオープンしたブラッセリー「ラ フォーレ」

木の仕上げで北欧らしさを演出したコペンハーゲン空港のショッピングエリア

シカゴ・オヘア空港の屋台ショップ

シンガポール・チャンギ空港の屋上プール

フランクフルト空港の第2ターミナル飲食プラザ中央に設けられた子供のための遊戯エリア

2 アミューズメント

巨大空港のハブ空港化などに伴い，滞留時間の長い旅客が増加してきた。旅客にとっては「物の消費」も楽しみなら，また空港の中での「時間の消費」も楽しいものだ。そのためのいろいろな施設や仕掛けが，格段に充実してきている。スキポール空港は先頃，ゴルフ練習場，日焼けサロン，フィットネスセンター，サウナなどを揃えたレジャー施設をオープンさせ，ついで，エアポートカジノも開設させた。トランジット客は，これで時間の使い方の選択肢が大きく広がった。ミュンヘン空港もディスコ，ゲームセンター，カジノとアミューズメント施設をふんだんに用意している。チャンギ空港の内容も濃い。フィットネス，サウナ，プール，小劇場（映画鑑賞），カラオケルーム，マッサージ，指圧と，至れり尽くせりの内容だ。

旅客をもてなすイベントに力を入れている空港も多い。フランクフルト空港では大道芸が披露され，時間待ちの客を楽しませている。またここでは，子供のための宇宙船のあるエリアがあり，ステージでは常時，音楽演奏や余興が行われている。スキポール空港は空港独自のテレビチャンネルを持っていて，250台のモニターが目を楽しませている。

ミュンヘン空港の一角にあるディスコ

ミュンヘン空港ターミナル内のカジノ

スキポール空港のトランジットエリアにあるゴルフ練習場

スキポール空港のフィットネスセンター

ビジネス客のためのちょっとしたコーナーの提供やビジネスを支援する諸々のサービスの提供といったレベルは，以前から空港には備わっていた。最近は，これに加えて本格的な会議室やオフィス，展示場まで備えた，いわゆるビジネスセンターの設置・運営へと進み，空港内におけるビジネスを巡る環境は大きく様変わりしている。

人と人，人と物が出会うのに最も合理性のある場としての空港の利便性，ビジネスチャンスの豊富さ，といった空港そのものの特性を生かして，空港をビジネスの拠点にしようという試みが，いま盛んに行われている。シャルル・ド・ゴール空港，フランクフルト空港など，世界の巨大空港は，ビジネス機能の強化に意欲的だ。

今後，空港と鉄道，高速道路とのネットワーク

3 ビジネスサポート

Business
Support

が完備されてくると，ビジネスのポテンシャルはますます大きく育っていくことだろう。空港周辺都市への経済的な波及効果も大いに期待されよう。また，空港自体も膨大な従業員を抱えた巨大な産業であり，空港の物流機能の強化なども伴い，ビジネス空間としての空港の可能性は大きいものがある。

ニース・コートダジュール空港は，現在はリゾート，観光といったイメージが強いが，ハイテク産業の立地を視野に入れ，空港をビジネス拠点化しようという構想を持っている。オーランド空港もディズニーワールドへの観光客が主体であったが，近年はビジネス機能の強化へとシフトしつつある。空港は地域にとって，ビジネスセンターとしての役割をより一層強めるだろう。

パリ・シャルル・ド・ゴール空港に建設中のビジネスセンターの中心をなすオフィスコンプレックス「ル・ドーム」

スキポール空港ターミナル内のビジネスセンター

ウィーン空港ターミナル前に新設されたワールドトレードセンター

ミュンヘン空港ターミナルに隣接するビジネスセンターの会議室

シンガポール・チャンギ空港にあるビジネスセンターのレセプション

空港が巨大化してくればくるほど，空間も機械的で複雑になり，味気ない印象になりがちである。そこで，空間をヒューマンなものに引き戻すために，花や緑，水や光，照明や空調，装飾やアート，イスや備品といった，ヒューマンスケールのもので構成することが重要になってくるのである。

アメニティの配慮と実践で最も進んでいるのはチャンギ空港であろう。「グリーン＆クリーン」をコンセプトに掲げて，内外を問わず，パブリックな空間は花と緑で埋め尽くし，旅客の心をなごませている。関西国際空港も旅客ターミナルビルの入り口，吹き抜け空間のキャニオンを緑の植栽で飾り，日本の鳥居をイメージしたという壁のベンガラ色とともに，心地よい空間をつくり出している。

明かりも重要である。多くの空港が陰影に富む間接照明を試みるなど，様々な対応を行っている。関西国際空港は，天井に帆の形をしたテフロンエアダクトが伸びているが，これは間接照明にもなり，やわらかな光の空間を提供している。デンバー空港のファイバーグラスの大屋根も，やわらかで心地よい自然光のシャワーを空間に降らせている。

ミュンヘン空港はアーティスティックなオブジェ

4 アメニティ

が至るところに展示され，空港自体がまるでモダン・ギャラリーといった趣になっている。フェニックス空港は招待アーチストの作品から学生や児童の作品まで，多くの展示エキシビションを，あたかも美術館のように空港内で行っている。

空港を語るときにイスは欠かすことができないものだ。極言すれば，空港はイスと通路とで成り立っているといえるぐらい，イスは空港の大切な基本設備である。空港のイスは膨大な数にのぼり，視覚的にも大きなボリュームを占める。ちなみに関西国際空港でのラウンジチェアは9000個を数えている。空港のイスは，適正な数，配置，用途（休憩用，待機用など），もちろん素材や形態，色にも細心の留意が必要だ。

コペンハーゲン空港は，定評あるスカンジナビアン・デザインの粋を尽くしたイスを揃えている。旅客を「ゲスト」ととらえるコペンハーゲン空港の理念がここにもよく表れている。帽子掛けやラッゲージ・カートなども心憎いデザインである。

ミュンヘン空港のラウンジチェアは，足置きが出て，リラックスできる。スキポール空港の鳥篭形の籐のイスやトランプのベンチは，ユーモアと洒落っ気にあふれている。

全米一のアートワーク展示数を誇るフェニックス・スカイハーバー空港

ミュンヘン空港の水を使ったアートワーク

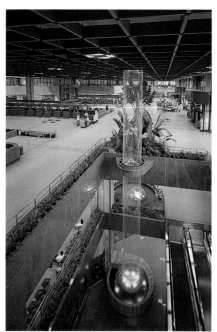
シンガポール・チャンギ空港ターミナル1の吹き抜けを貫くオブジェ

デンバー空港メーンターミナル内の植栽

旅客のリラクセーションを考慮したミュンヘン空港のラウンジチェア

フロリダの亜熱帯植物に覆われたオーランド空港のパーキングビル

ロッキー山脈の山並みをデザインモチーフにしたデンバー空港のターミナル膜屋根

コペンハーゲン空港の広報担当者は,「国際空港はお国自慢のディスプレイ」だと述べている。空港はまさしくその国や地域の,文化・歴史・伝統・自然・産業をアピールする,格好の場である。アイデンティティを空港で表現することは,地域経営が自立を求め,世界との交流や連携を深めれば深めるほど,重要な意味を持ってこよう。国や文化・自然を最もストレートにわかりやすく表現したのが,インドネシアのスカルノ・ハッタ空港やヌグアライ空港である。前者は庭園空港として伝統的なインドネシア建築を,後者はバリの伝統的デザインをモチーフにして,現地の職人により細部に至る装飾まで,忠実に見事に再現している。飛行機が駐機していなければ,本物の伝統建築に見まごうほどだ。ここを訪れる人には,強いインパクトを与えるであろう。特に,観光に重点を置いている地域の空港では,このようなアイデンティティのストレートな表現は効果的であろう。

5 ローカル・アイデンティティ

Local
Identity

フェニックス空港は,アリゾナのリゾート空港にふさわしく,カーペットや壁のレリーフなどに先住民族の幾何学模様をデザインしている。音楽の都と称されるオーストリアのウィーン空港は,ターミナルの平面プランがバイオリンの弦柱頭を形どったものとなっている。デンバー空港は背景のロッキー山脈の山並みをデザインモチーフにした個性的な外観で話題となっている。関西国際空港のターミナルビルも,日本建築の明るさと軽さを表現した空間構成や,ターミナルビルの広大なエンドウォールのガラス面から見える竹藪は,日本の心象風景を表現したものといえよう。

周辺の生態系や景観との協調・調和など,空港にとってエコロジーも大きなテーマである。オーランド空港は周辺の湿地帯との調和を,ミュンヘン空港は周辺の田園風景との調和をそれぞれ重視したランドスケープを実現した。

庭園空港をコンセプトに,緑の中にインドネシアの伝統建築を配したジャカルタ・スカルノ・ハッタ空港

伝統的な意匠が各所に配されたジャカルタ・スカルノ・ハッタ空港ターミナル

職人の手による伝統装飾が施されたヌグアライ空港フェスティバルプラザ

トンネル内に多彩なアートワークを施したデンバー空港のターミナルシャトル

生態系保護を図った湿地帯の間を走るオーランド空港のターミナルシャトル

海上空港である関西空港へは特急電車や車のほか、海上から高速船ジェットフォイルでもアクセスできる

パリ・シャルル・ド・ゴール空港の搭乗ゲートから遠隔エプロンの航空機にアクセスする高さ調節可能なモービルラウンジ

空港の備えるべき機能で，最も大切で基本的なものは，旅客のスムーズな移動の確保である。これは空港外の周辺都市と空港との多様でスムーズなアクセスの確保と，空港内での，旅客の短い歩行距離と明快な動線確保である。

この機能の追求は，いつの時代の空港も，またどんな規模の空港も，最重点に行われなければならない。近年は高速鉄道や高速道路など，空港と周辺都市とのモビリティの高速化，多様化が進行しつつある。車や列車から空港ターミナルへ，そして飛行機へと，旅客のスムーズな移動は空港にとって，その時代の最先端の技術が使われる，最大の課題である。

特に近年は，空港が巨大化しているため，空港内の移動も多様な解決が図られている。これまでタテの移動を担ってきたエスカレーターやエ

6 モビリティ

Mobility

レベーターに加え，ヨコの移動として，動く歩道やAGT，循環バスなどが多く導入されている。スキポール空港は，新設のスキポールプラザの地階に国鉄駅が直結しており，18分でアムステルダムの中心街に着く。また国内の他都市やドイツ，フランス，ベルギーの主要都市へも直通または1回の乗り換えで行くことができるのが強みだ。さらに，今世紀末には駅は拡張され，ヨーロッパ高速鉄道システム（TGV）に加わる予定である。シャルル・ド・ゴール空港はインターモダル・コンプレックス（航空機，TGV，郊外電車，空港内ピープル・ムーバーの全てのネットワークの基地）が設けられている。ミュンヘン空港も鉄道空港といわれるように，鉄道との結合に重点を置いている。

シカゴ・オヘア空港のコンコース間を結ぶトンネルのムービングサイドウオーク

スキポール空港のプラザ地階に直結するオランダ国鉄駅

空港が通常のホテルやデパートと異なるのは，老若男女のみならず，国籍や文化を異にする，多くの人々が，昼夜の別なく利用せざるを得ないということである。そのため，社会的弱者の救済を始めとして，想定しうるあらゆるトラブルに対応する，万全の設備や体勢を整えておく必要がある。

コペンハーゲン空港が，空港のホスピタリティ精神をうまく言い表わしている。「旅客一人の問題はわれわれ全員の問題」。コペンハーゲン空港では，このような考え方が，施設面にもオペレーション面にも貫かれている。

ホスピタリティの施設や設備として，一般的には，託児所や病院，教会，車イスや荷物用カート，子供のための水飲み場などがあげられよう。

7 ホスピタリティ

Hospitality

ウィーン空港は24時間体制の医療設備を用意している。フランクフルト空港は，世界のあらゆる宗教に対応できるような祈とう・瞑想室を揃えているのが興味深い。デンバー空港は水飲み場の高さが3段階になっていて，子供や体の不自由な人にも楽に利用できるようになっている。ラウンジもホスピタリティのための施設としてとらえれば，客層や利用形態によって，様々なきめ細かな対応が考えられる。

セキュリティ確保も空港での必須条件だ。特に近年は，ハードな施設で対応する方策に加え，人々の目による相互のチェックなどのソフトセキュリティの考え方も大きく取り入れられており，この面からも見通しのきく大空間がセキュリティ面に大きな機能を持ってくる。

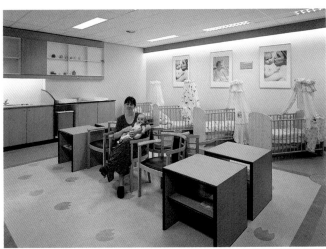

スキポール空港ターミナル内の託児所

パリ・シャルル・ド・ゴール空港ターミナル1の教会

車椅子用にレベル差をつけたデンバー空港のセンサー付き水飲み場

パスポートコントロールを経た後に使うコペンハーゲン空港の手荷物用カートとベビーカー

チューリッヒ空港ターミナル各所には車椅子用バッテリー充電器が備え付けられている

空港の通路や広場は，いまや単なる無機質の空間ではなく，メディアスペースへと大きく変貌している。そしてその名も，アトリウムやプラザ，コンコース，広場などと呼ばれ，様々な展示やインフォメーションが行われ，多種多様な店舗が取り巻くコミュニケーションの空間となっている。

旅客を誘導する最も効果的なサインは旅客の案内を空間そのものに委ねることで，自分が今どこにいるか，これからどこに行かなくてはならないかを，直接自分の目で知ることである。そ

8 コミュニケーション

Com-
munication

こは，ちょうど大都市の街角のように，人々の待ち合わせの場であるとともに，一つの大きなサインとしての意味合いを持っているのである。アトリウムやプラザは，まさしく空港の情報軸として，重要な位置づけにあるとの認識で計画される必要があるだろう。

そのコミュニケーションスペースを演出し支える装置が，電話，サイン，スピーカー，インフォメーションボード等々であり，そのデザインや機能は大いに吟味されなくてはならない。

デンバー空港メーンターミナルのインフォメーションボード

航空機のエンジンのエアインテークを模したウィーン空港のインフォメーションモニター

スキポール空港プラザ内のミーティングポイント

有名なチボリ公園をデザインモチーフにしたコペンハーゲン空港のショップサイン

ローカルアイデンティティを意識したジャカルタ・スカルノ・ハッタ空港のテレフォンブース

デンバー空港のテレフォンブース

空港データ

アムステルダム・スキポール空港データ（P10）

●ベーシックデータ

空港名：アムステルダム・スキポール空港
Amsterdam Airport Schiphol
コード：AMS
空港アドレス：1118 ZG, Schiphol Airport, The Netherlands
開港年：1967年5月

●空港概要

空港敷地面積：約2000ha
滑走路本数：5本
（長さ3400m，幅45m）×1
（長さ3300m，幅45m）×1
（長さ3250m，幅45m）×1
（長さ3450m，幅45m）×1
（長さ2018m，幅45m）×1
エプロン数：7
スポット数：124
シティセンターまでの距離：17km
同アクセス時間：電車／17分

●フライトデータ（1994年）

年間離発着回数：29万9712回
年間旅客数：国際線／2294万2979人 国内線／12万6386人　トランジット／49万0091人　合計／2355万9456人
年間貨物取扱量：合計／83万8127トン

●ターミナル概要

ターミナル数：3（西ターミナル，中央ターミナル，南ターミナル）
主な施設およびアメニティスペース：スキポールプラザ，アートギャラリー，託児所，ビジネスセンター，国営カジノ，フィットネスセンター，ゴルフセンター，トランジットホテル，サウナ，日焼けサロンなど
駐車場収容台数：1万6566台

ウィーン国際空港データ（P22）

●ベーシックデータ

空港名：ウィーン国際空港
Vienna international Airport
コード：VIE
運営管理者：Flughafen Wien AG／Dr. Gerhard Kastelic and Dr. Franz Kotrba
空港アドレス：A-1300 Wien-Flughafen, P.O. Box 1, Austria
開港年：1954年

●空港概要

空港敷地面積：約1000ha
滑走路本数：2本
（長さ3000m，幅45m）×1
（長さ3600m，幅45m）×1
スポット数：73
シティセンターまでの距離：16km
同アクセス時間：車・リムジンバス／15〜20分，電車／30分

●フライトデータ（1994年）

年間離発着回数（回）：

	国際線	国内線	計
到着便／	57,000	6,000	6万3000回
出発便／	57,000	6,000	6万3000回

年間旅客数（人）：

	国際線	国内線	計
到着便	3,576,000	186,000	376万2000人
出発便	3,584,000	178,000	376万2000人
トランジット	206,000	—	20万6000人

年間貨物取扱量（トン）：

	国際線	国内線	計
到着便／	42,171	307	4万2478トン
出発便／	39,455	679	4万0134トン

乗り入れ航空会社数：国際線／61
国内線／5　チャーター便／122
合計／188

●ターミナル概要

ターミナル数：2
（ターミナル1，ターミナル2）
構造：RC造
規模：ターミナル1／3層
ターミナル2／4層
主な設計者名：Prof. Dipl. Ing. Franz Fehringer
主な施工者名：ARGE Universale-Eborhard-Porr.

●コンセッション

テナント数：物販／53　飲食／16
合計／69
テナント部分延べ床面積：物販／4454m²
飲食／6389m²
主なテナント：デューティーフリーショップ，レストラン，スペシャリティショップ（オーストリア製品／スワロフスキー，デーメルなど　インターナショナルブランド／タイ・ラック，キャビア・ハウス，ボディ・ショップ，ハロッズなど）

ミュンヘン空港データ（P30）

●ベーシックデータ

空港名：ミュンヘン空港
Flughafen München
コード：MUC
運営管理者：Flughafen München, Willi Hermssen, Walter Vill, Klaus Brendlin
空港アドレス：Postfach 23 17 55, 85326 München, Germany
開港年月日：1992年5月17日

●空港概要

空港敷地面積：1500ha
滑走路本数：2本
（長さ4000m，幅60m）×2本
エプロン数：5
シティセンターまでの距離：28.5km
同アクセス時間：車・リムジンバス／約40分　地下鉄／38分

●フライトデータ（1994年）

年間離発着回数（回）：

	国際線	国内線	計
到着便	56,106	38,072	9万4178回
出発便	56,630	37,563	9万4193回

年間旅客数（人）：

	国際線	国内線	計
到着便	4,144,477	2,485,384	662万9861人
出発便	4,146,907	2,475,071	662万1978人
トランジット	—	—	24万5202人

年間貨物取扱量（トン）：

	国際線	国内線	計
到着便／	25,708	17,253	4万2961トン
出発便／	30,009	21,253	5万1262トン
トランジット／	—	—	8,379トン

乗り入れ航空会社数：103

●ターミナル概要

ターミナル数：1
延べ床面積：20万m²
主な設計者名：Prof. Hans-Busso von Busse, Prof. Eberhard Stauβ
主な施設およびアメニティスペース：カジノ，ディスコ，ヘアサロンなど

●コンセッション

テナント数：132
テナント部分延べ床面積：7600m²

シンガポール・チャンギ空港データ（P42）

●ベーシックデータ

空港名：シンガポール・チャンギ空港
Singapore Changi Airport
コード：SIN
運営管理者：Civil Aviation Authority of Singapore
空港アドレス：PO Box 1, Singapore Changi Airport, Singapore 918141
開港年月日：1981年7月1日

●空港概要

空港敷地面積：1300ha
滑走路本数：2本
（長さ4000m，幅60m）×2
スポット数：83
シティセンターまでの距離：20km
同アクセス時間：車・リムジンバス／20分

●フライトデータ（1994年）

年間離発着回数：
到着便／7万2565回　出発便／7万2769回
年間旅客数：到着便／1013万4100人
出発便／1006万8537人
トランジット／144万2040人
年間貨物取扱量：
到着便／52万9334トン
出発便／48万0430トン
乗り入れ航空会社数：65

●ターミナル概要

ターミナル数：2
（ターミナル1，ターミナル2）
構造：RC造
規模：4層
ターミナル間のアクセス：シャトルバス＆スカイトレイン
延べ床面積：ターミナル1／20万20m²
ターミナル2／28万5000m²
合計／48万5020m²
主な設計者名：Airport Development Division (Public Works Division)
主な施工者名：Takenaka Construction
主な施設およびアメニティスペース：ビジネスセンター，サウナ，フィットネスセンター，ヘアサロン，託児所，サイエンスディスカバリーセンター，トランジットホテル，スイミングプール，ジャクジー，インフォメーションセンター，チルドレンプレイエリアなど

●コンセッション

テナント数：65
主なテナント：書店・雑誌・文具，チョコレート＆キャンディ，CD，コンピューター・ソフトウエア＆ハードウエア，デリカテッセン，デューティーフリーショップ，ファッションウエア＆皮革製品，生花，ギフト＆ノベルティグッズ，工芸品＆みやげ物，ジュエリー，家電製品，時計・眼鏡，香水・コスメティック，陶器・クリスタル，カメラ・フィルム，スポーツ用品，玩具・ゲームなど

デンバー国際空港データ（P52）

●ベーシックデータ
空港名：デンバー国際空港
Denver International Airport
コード：DEN
運営管理者：City & Country of Denver, Dept. of Aviation
空港アドレス：8500 Peña Boulevard, Denver, Colorado 80249-6340, U.S.A.
開港年月日：1995年2月28日
●空港概要
空港敷地面積：約1万3759.7ha
滑走路本数：5本
（長さ3650m，幅45m）×5
ゲート数：94
シティセンターまでの距離：40km
同アクセス時間：車・リムジンバス／30分
●フライトデータ
年間離発着回数：53万0839回
年間旅客数：到着便／1658万9168人
出発便／1654万4260人
年間貨物取扱量：38万1233トン
乗り入れ航空会社数：18
●ターミナル概要
ターミナル数：4（メーンターミナル1，エアサイドコンコース3）
ターミナル間のアクセス：シャトルトレイン（AGT），ムービングサイドウォーク
主な設計者名：C.W.Fentress J.H. Bradburn and Associates, P.C.
主な施工者名：Morrison Knudsen & Greiner Engineering
●コンセッション
テナント数：物販／107
テナント部分延べ床面積：1万8580m²

シカゴ・オヘア国際空港データ（P64）

●ベーシックデータ
空港名：シカゴ・オヘア国際空港
Chicago O'Hare International Airport
コード：ORD
運営管理者：City of Chicago, Department of Aviation
空港アドレス：AMF O'Hare,P.O.Box 66142,Chicago, Illinois 60666 U.S.A.
開港年：1949年
●空港概要
空港敷地面積：3116ha
滑走路本数：6本
（長さ4000m，幅60m）×1
（長さ3100m，幅45m）×2
（長さ2600m，幅45m）×1 ほか
シティセンターまでの距離：約27km
同アクセス時間：車，リムジンバス／35〜60分 地下鉄，鉄道／35〜45分
●フライトデータ（1994年）
年間離発着回数：88万3062回
年間旅客数：6646万8269人
年間貨物取扱量：138万4613トン
乗り入れ航空会社数：60
●ターミナル概要
ターミナル数：4（ターミナル1，2，3，5）※ターミナル5は国際線専用
ターミナル間のアクセス：シャトルトレイン（AGT）
主な施設概要：レストラン，スナックバー，コーヒーバー，ニューススタンド，ギフトショップなどのコンセッション施設，エアポートホテル（ヒルトンホテル），郵便局，医務室，教会，歯科医院，両替所，ビジネスセンター，

UICメディカルセンターなど

フェニックス・スカイハーバー国際空港データ（P72）

●ベーシックデータ
空港名：フェニックス・スカイハーバー国際空港
Phoenix Sky Harbor International Airport
コード：PHX
運営管理者：City of Phoenix Aviation Department
空港アドレス：3400 Sky Harbor Blvd., Phoenix, AZ 85034, U.S.A.
開港年月日：1935年7月16日
●空港概要
空港敷地面積：903.2ha
滑走路本数：2本
（長さ3350m，幅45m）×1
（長さ3140m，幅45m）×1
ゲート数：90
シティセンターまでの距離：8km
同アクセス時間：車・リムジンバス／12分
●フライトデータ（1994年）
年間離発着回数（回）：
　　　　国際線　国内線　　計
到着便／17,000　511,000　52万8000回
出発便／20,000　520,000　54万0000回
年間旅客数（人）：
　　　国際線　国内線　　計
　183,132　25,443,000　2562万6132人
年間貨物取扱量：25万7418トン
乗り入れ航空会社数：17
●ターミナル概要
ターミナル数：4（ターミナル2〜4，貴賓用ターミナル）
規模：ターミナル2／2層
ターミナル3，4／3層
延べ床面積：32万5160m²
主な設計者名：City of Phoenix Aviation Department, Planning and Development Division
主な施工者名：City of Phoenix Aviation Department, Planning and Development Division
駐車場収容台数：1万261台
●コンセッション
テナント数：64
テナント総売り上げ：2070万1981 US$（約20億7019万円）

パリ・シャルル・ド・ゴール空港データ（P80）

●ベーシックデータ
空港名：シャルル・ド・ゴール空港
Charles de Gaulle Airport
コード：CDG
運営管理者：Aéroports de Paris(ADP)
空港アドレス：291,Boulevard Raspaie E75675 Paris Cedex 14, France
開港：1974年10月24日
●空港概要
空港敷地面積：3109ha
滑走路本数：2本
（長さ3600m，幅60m）×2
シティセンターまでの距離：27km
同アクセス時間：車／45分 電車／30分
●フライトデータ（1994年）
年間離発着回数：国際線／28万0861回
国内線／3万7857回 合計／31万8718回
年間旅客数：国際線／2569万0024人
国内線／267万2748人

合計／2836万2772人
年間貨物取扱量：国際線／74万6195トン 国内線／4万0097トン
合計／78万6292トン
乗り入れ航空会社数：80
●ターミナル概要
ターミナル数：3（CDG1,CDG2,T9）
※T9はチャーター便専用ターミナル
ターミナル間のアクセス：シャトルバス
延べ床面積：CDG1／23万1100m²
CDG2／20万m² T9／8200m²
合計　43万9300m²
主な設計者名：Paul Andreu
●コンセッション
テナント数：78
テナント総売り上げ：
29億8775仏フラン（約657億3050万円）

コペンハーゲン空港データ（P90）

●ベーシックデータ
空港名：コペンハーゲン空港
Copenhagen Airport
コード：CPH
運営管理者：Copenhagen Airport A/S
空港アドレス：Flyvervej 11, DK-2770 Kastrup, Denmark
開港年月日：1925年4月20日
●空港概要
空港敷地面積：1240ha
滑走路本数：3本
（長さ3600m，幅45m）×1
（長さ3300m，幅45m）×1
（長さ2800m，幅45m）×1
エプロン数：5
スポット数：70
シティセンターまでの距離：8km
同アクセス時間：車・リムジンバス／15〜20分
●フライトデータ（1994年）
年間離発着回数：国際線／17万8149回
国内線／5万0360回 合計／22万8509回
年間旅客数：国際線／1149万5000人
国内線／257万8785人
合計／1407万3785人
年間貨物取扱量：27万3505トン
乗り入れ航空会社数：60
●ターミナル概要
ターミナル数：2（国際線ターミナル，国内線ターミナル）
ターミナル間のアクセス：シャトルバス
規模：地上3階地下1階建て
延べ床面積：合計 8万6000m²
主な設計者名：Vilhelm Laurttzen Succ.
●コンセッション
テナント数：35
テナント部分延べ床面積：3200m²
主なテナント：デューティーフリーショップ，レストラン，スペシャリティショップ（ロイヤルコペンハーゲン，ジョージ・ジェンセン，バイキング時代のジュエリーを忠実に再現したレプリカを販売するミュージアム・コピーショップなど）ほか

ジャカルタ・スカルノ・ハッタ国際空港データ（P98）

●ベーシックデータ
空港名：ジャカルタ・スカルノ・ハッタ国際空港
Jakarta Soekarno-Hatta International Airport
コード：CGK

運営管理者：Autonomous Airport Authority；P.T.Angkasa Pura II
空港アドレス：Jakarta International Airport Soekarno-Hatta BLD 601, Jakarta 19101, Indonesia
開港年：1984年10月
●空港概要
空港敷地面積：1800ha
滑走路本数：2本
（長さ3660m，幅60m）×1本
（長さ3600m，幅60m）×1本
エプロン数：12
シティセンターまでの距離：23km
同アクセス時間：車・リムジンバス／45分
●フライトデータ
年間離発着回数（回）：
　　　　国際線　国内線　　計
到着便／17,800　52,400　7万0200回
出発便／17,900　52,400　7万0300回
年間旅客数（人）：
　　　　国際線　国内線　　計
到着便2,324,500 3,815,500 614万0000人
出発便2,363,400 3,739,600 610万3000人
トランジット188,000 233,000 42万1000人
年間貨物取扱量（トン）：
　　　　国際線　国内線　　計
到着便／52,724　37,318　9万0042トン
出発便／97,980　57,284　15万5264トン
乗り入れ航空会社数：36
●ターミナル概要
ターミナル数：2
（ターミナル1，ターミナル2）
ターミナル間のアクセス：シャトルバス
構造：RC造
延べ床面積：ターミナル1／12万5000m²
ターミナル2／15万1308m²
合計／27万6308m²
主な設計者名：Aéroports de Paris, Paul Andreu-Architect,
主な施工者名：Consortium of French Contractors：Saint Rapt et Brice, Colas, Societe Auxiliaire d'Enterprises Consortium of Indonesian Contractors：P.T. Konavi, P.T. Cakar Bumi, P.T. Dacrea Avia
●コンセッション
テナント数：146
テナント総売り上げ：390万5329 US$（約3億9053万円）
テナント総賃料：681万5692 US$（約6億8157万円）
主なテナント：デューティーフリーショップ，レストラン，ファストフード，スナックバー，銀行，両替所，保険エージェント，ショップ（バティックほかの民芸品，銀細工，彫刻，革製品など）

チューリッヒ空港データ（P104）

●ベーシックデータ
空港名：チューリッヒ空港
Zürich Airport
コード：ZRH
運営管理者：Zürich Airport Authority
空港アドレス：CH-8058 Zürich Airport, Switzerland
開港年月日：1948年11月17日
●空港概要
空港敷地面積：807ha
滑走路本数：3本
（長さ2500m，幅60m）×1本
（長さ3300m，幅60m）×1本
（長さ3700m，幅60m）×1本
スポット数：56

170